T0318992

Cambridge Elements ≡

Elements in Music and Musicians 1750–1850
edited by
Simon P. Keefe
University of Sheffield

DR CHARLES BURNEY AND THE ORGAN

Pierre Dubois, Souvigny

CAMBRIDGE
UNIVERSITY PRESS

CAMBRIDGE
UNIVERSITY PRESS

University Printing House, Cambridge CB2 8BS, United Kingdom

One Liberty Plaza, 20th Floor, New York, NY 10006, USA

477 Williamstown Road, Port Melbourne, VIC 3207, Australia

314–321, 3rd Floor, Plot 3, Splendor Forum, Jasola District Centre,
New Delhi – 110025, India

79 Anson Road, #06–04/06, Singapore 079906

Cambridge University Press is part of the University of Cambridge.

It furthers the University's mission by disseminating knowledge in the pursuit of
education, learning, and research at the highest international levels of excellence.

www.cambridge.org
Information on this title: www.cambridge.org/9781108972864
DOI: 10.1017/9781108973212

First published 2021

A catalogue record for this publication is available from the British Library.

ISBN 978-1-108-97286-4 Paperback
ISSN 2732-558X (online)
ISSN 2732-5571 (print)

Dr Charles Burney and the Organ

Elements in Music and Musicians 1750–1850

DOI: 10.1017/9781108973212
First published online: February 2021

Pierre Dubois, Souvigny (France)
Author for correspondence: Pierre Dubois, pierdubois@wanadoo.fr

Abstract: Whereas Dr Burney's writings are often mentioned in studies on eighteenth-century music, not much interest seems to have been given specifically to his relation to the organ, which played an important part in his professional career as a practising musician. No better introduction to the aesthetic ethos of the eighteenth-century English organ can be found than in Burney's remarks disseminated in his various writings. Taken together, they construct a coherent discourse on taste and constitute an aesthetic. Burney's view of the organ is indicative of a broader ethos of moderation that permeates his whole work and is at one with the dominant moral philosophy of Georgian England. This conception is ripe with patriotic undertones, while it also articulates a constant plea for politeness as a condition for harmonious social interaction. He believed that moderation, simplicity and fancy were the constituents of good taste as well as good manners.

Keywords: music, organ, moderation, manners, Dr Charles Burney

ISBNs: 9781108972864 (PB), 9781108973212 (OC)
ISSNs: 2732-558X (online), 2732-5571 (print)

Contents

Introduction

Charles Burney (see Figure 1) is mainly known today for his outstanding contribution to the history of music. His initial training was that of a musician, and more specifically that of a harpsichordist and organist. His project of writing a *General History of Music from the earliest ages to the present Period*, published in four volumes between 1776 (the very year of the publication of John Hawkins's rival *General History of the Science and Practice of Music*) and 1789, originated in his deep personal interest in music, of course, but also in his wish to raise himself above the status of practising musician and to become a 'man of letters'. His ambition was to 'bridge ... the considerable gulf that separated the musician from the world of polite letters'.[1] His success was confirmed by his acceptance within the circle of Henry and Hester Lynch Thrale at Streatham Park,[2] and he took pride in his contacts and exchanges with numerous writers in England as well as abroad (Dr Johnson, Garrick, Twining, Mason, Metastasio, Padre Martini, Rousseau, Diderot and Voltaire, to name but a few).

Whereas Dr Burney's writings are often referred to and quoted in studies on eighteenth-century music, it is somewhat paradoxical that not much interest seems to have been given specifically to his relation to the organ, on which he was a proficient performer, and which played an important part in his professional career as a practising musician. Burney's love of the organ, which he called 'that most comprehensive of all instruments' (*History* II, 423), appears to have been deep, sincere and lasting. As Percy A. Scholes noted, 'the organ provided a background to Burney's whole musical life'.[3] As we shall see, Burney maintained a position as an organist in various churches throughout his life and, in the course of his travels abroad, he never missed an opportunity to visit organs of interest.

Burneyan scholarship has rightly been dominated by Roger Lonsdale's *Dr Charles Burney, a Literary Biography* and Percy A. Scholes's *The Great Dr Burney*.[4] Lawrence Lipking also provided a very interesting interpretation of the epistemological significance of Burney's *History of Music* in his study *The Ordering of the Arts in Eighteenth-Century England*.[5] These wide-ranging

---

[1] Roger Lonsdale, *Dr Charles Burney, a Literary Biography* (Oxford: The Clarendon Press, 1965), 108.

[2] Valerie Rumbold, 'Music Aspires to Letters: Charles Burney, Queeney Thrale and the Streatham Circle', *Music & Letters*, vol. 74, no. 1 (Feb., 1993), 24–38, 24.

[3] Percy A. Scholes, *A New Enquiry into the Life and Work of Dr Burney* (London: Proceedings of the Musical Association, Session LXVII, 1941), 1–30.

[4] Percy A. Scholes's *The Great Dr Burney* (London, New York, Toronto: Oxford University Press, 1948).

[5] Lawrence Lipking, *The Ordering of the Arts in Eighteenth-Century England* (Princeton, New Jersey: Princeton University Press, 1970).

Figure 1 George Dance, *Charles Burney*, pencil, 1794. © London, National Portrait Gallery

works occasionally mention Burney's interest in the organ, but, understandably, they do not pay particular attention to this aspect of his activity. Burney's numerous writings (the *History of Music*, the accounts of his travels on the continent to collect material for the former, numerous remarks in his personal papers and letters, his *Account of the Commemoration of Handel*, and his contribution to Rees's *Cyclopedia*, for which he wrote the chapter on the organ) provide a unique wealth of information that can greatly contribute to helping us figure out the way the organ was conceived in the English eighteenth-century psyche. In this Element, I endeavour to capture Burney's views on the organ as a musical instrument and to outline his conception of the qualities required in both the organ and organists.

However, this Element encompasses a broader range of issues than those simply concerning its main protagonist, Dr Burney, and his favourite instrument. Taken together, Burney's remarks on the organ, organists and organ music construct a coherent discourse on taste and constitute an aesthetic. They also enable a 'reading' of English society in the eighteenth century through the magnifying glass of one particular musical instrument, the organ, for, as we shall see, Burney's view of the organ is indicative of a broader ethos of moderation that permeates his whole work and is at one with the dominant moral philosophy of Georgian England. This conception is ripe with patriotic undertones, while it also articulates a constant plea for politeness as a condition for harmonious social interaction. The underlying assumption of our approach is that musical instruments help construct an *imaginaire*, or imagined representation of the world, that is ripe with aesthetic, social and ethical meanings that go well beyond their purely musical functions or roles. By tracing the evolution of the English organ back to the Restoration and setting Burney's remarks on the instrument in their historical context, it is possible to see how the instrument and its repertoire reflected the social and philosophical ideals of Georgian England.

1 Burney, the Professional Organist

The 'first Music he [Burney] learned was of Mr Baker the Organist of the Cathedral [of Chester] who being distressed for an assistant during a fit of the Gout, taught [him] to play a Chant on the Organ before he knew his Gamut or the names of the keys', Burney wrote in the manuscript memoirs of his life (*Memoirs*, 23). The young boy soon learned to play a few more chants and a few songs by Handel, 'wch he performed without knowing a word of Italian or hardly a note of Music'. He then pursued his musical studies under his half-brother James Burney, organist of St Mary's, Shrewsbury. James, Burney explained, 'had a very good finger, & what he attempted, wch was neither very brilliant nor elaborate he executed neatly. He had however, no application for the slavery of conquering difficulties in the Lessons of the Times; & his want of Licence as well as fancy prevented his Voluntaries from rising above poverty & common-place' (*Memoirs*, 33). By contrast, when 'the Celebrated Felton, from Hereford, & after him the 1st Dr Hayes, from Oxford, came to Shrewsbury on a Tour', the young Charles Burney was 'struck & stimulated ... so forcibly by their performance on the Organ as well as encouragm^t that [he] went to work with an ambition & fury that w^d hardly allow [him] to eat or sleep'. He then went back to Chester where, in 1744, the organist and composer Thomas Augustine Arne (1710–78), on his way back from Dublin to London, offered to take him as an apprentice, to which Charles's father consented. Burney accompanied his master to London and worked very hard for him, transcribing music and playing in various orchestras, without any personal pecuniary profit but learning much through first-hand experience, until the eccentric, wealthy and refined Fulke Greville (1717–1806), Member of Parliament and High Sheriff of Wiltshire, took an interest in him and released him from his apprenticeship by hiring him in 1746. In 1753, Burney was to write a poem dedicated to Fulke Greville, in which he evoked the most famous English composers of the time (*Letters*, 'To Fulke Greville': King's Lynn, July 1753).

Once his initial training was over, Charles Burney acquired various successive positions as an organist. In 1749, aged twenty-three and with a young wife and child to support, he paid the fees to become a Freeman of the Musicians' Company,[6] and applied for the post of organist of St Dionis Backchurch,[7] with an annual salary of £30, succeeding the renowned organist and composer Philip Hart, who had been involved in the designing of the church's organ. Burney was elected with a huge majority of fifty votes, 'followed by Gilding (afterwards organist of St Edmund the King and Martyr, Lombard Street) with four, Larkin with one, and the other six with none at all',[8] which is an indication of Burney's proficiency on the organ. He was officially appointed on 26 October 1749 and was to retain this position until his resignation in 1752, when he was succeeded by John Bennett.[9] St Dionis Backchurch was a small, wealthy parish church in the Langbourn ward of the City of London (see Figure 2).[10] The church had been built to the design of Christopher Wren after the Great Fire of London, when, owing to the growing population of London, Parliament had passed an act in 1711 for the building of fifty new churches in the City of London and Westminster.[11]

The organ had originally been built by Renatus Harris in 1724,[12] and approved by a board of experts including Croft, Handel and Loeillet.[13] As Richard Pratt has shown, the contract (which is still preserved) is quite similar to that of the Gerard Smith organ for St George's Hanover Square, built at the same time (1724–25).[14] Harris had a great reputation and this may be why Gerard Smith's project closely followed the specification of the organ at St Dionis Backchurch. This organ, the last instrument built by Renatus Harris, had three manuals and 1,541 pipes, and cost £585.[15] It was probably an 'influential instrument' at the time, which set 'a new model for organs in wealthy parish churches', as Stephen Bicknell has remarked.[16] In particular, one can notice the French influence in the mutations on the Great and the proliferation and variety

[6] See Donovan Dawe, *The Organists of the City of London, 1666–1850: a Record of One-Thousand Organists* (Padstow: Donovan Dawe, 1983), 12.

[7] Lonsdale, *Dr Charles Burney*, 23.

[8] Parish records, mentioned by F. G. Edwards, *Musical Times*, July 1904. See Scholes, *The Great Dr Burney*, vol. I, 51.

[9] See Dawe, *Organists of the City of London*, 39.

[10] See 'St Dionis Backchurch', in www.londonlives.org/static/StDionisBackchurch.jsp.

[11] It was demolished in 1878. A photograph of the organ case (*c*.1870) held in the National Historic Archive is reproduced in Stephen Bicknell, *The History of the English Organ* (Cambridge: Cambridge University Press, 1996), 159.

[12] See James Boeringer, *Organa Britannica – Organs in Great Britain 1660–1860* (Lewisburg, PA: Bucknell University Press, 1986), vol. II, 164–6.

[13] Richard Platt, 'Plagiarism or Emulation: the Gerard Smith Organ Contract for St George's Church, Hanover Square', *BIOS Journal*, no. 17 (1997), 32–46, 40; Bicknell, *History of the English Organ*, 157.

[14] Platt, 'Plagiarism or Emulation', 32.

[15] Nicholas M. Plumley, *The Organs of the City of London* (Oxford: Positif Press, 1996), 147.

[16] Bicknell, *History of the English Organ*, 157.

Figure 2 George Shepherd, *View of St Dionis Backchurch*, 1811, Crace
XXIII.30. © The Trustees of the British Museum

of the reed stops (ten out of twenty-five stops in all), intended to imitate as well
as possible the original sounds of the human voice and the instruments after
which the stops were named. The aim was imitative variety, which 'provided the
background for the habits of organists' in England in the eighteenth century, as
the 'sounds of the English organ were partly related to the character of contemporary instrumental playing'.[17] Harris's organs were reputed for their fullness
and smoothness of tone (as opposed to the brilliance of Father Smith's organs)
and they paved the way for the delicate and sophisticated sound of late Georgian
organs (such as those of Samuel Green, in particular). The organ was rather new

---

[17] Bicknell, *History of the English Organ*, 162.

when the young Burney was appointed at St Dionis Backchurch. It must have been quite a sensational instrument of which to be in charge, and one can surmise that it contributed substantially to the shaping of Burney's own taste in organs (Table 1).

Soon after his election at St Dionis Backchurch, Burney was also appointed to replace the blind organist and composer John Stanley for a new concert series at the King's Arms Tavern, which replaced the concerts previously held at the Swan Tavern after the latter was destroyed by the great fire in Cornhill in 1748.[18] Stanley and Sir Joseph Hankey, who ran the initial series, had quarrelled, and so Burney was chosen to preside at the organ and harpsichord, which he undertook 'with fear and trembling, being always extremely timid in public playing'. On the very first night, he executed an organ concerto of his own composition, 'in w^{ch} [he] had not forgotten the sweetness of the Hautbois stop in the Adagio, wch by means of the swell and accompaniments of the [*blank*] happened to please', as he explained in his *Memoirs* (*Memoirs*, 91). Following a fashion introduced by Handel, the organ concerto had acquired a particular significance in England. William Mason wrote that Handel's intention in

Table 1 St Dionis Backchurch: Stop list*

Great	Choir	Swell
Open Diapason	Open Diapason to mid-C	Open Diapason
Stop^d Diapason	Stop^d Diapason to gamut	Stop^d Diapason
Principal	Principal	Principal
Twelfth	Flute	Cornet III
Fifteenth	Fifteenth	Trumpet
Tierce	Bassoon	Cremona
Larigot	French Horn to D	Vox Humana
Sesquialtera IV	Cremona (from Great)	
Trumpet	Clarion (from Great)	
Cremona or French Horn		
Clarion		
Cornet V		

* From Bicknell, *The History of the English Organ*, 158; *The Leffler Manuscript* (c.1802–16), facsimile edition with introduction by Peter Williams (Reigate: B. I. O. S., 2010), 192. Leffler attributed the building of the organ to Byfield, Bridge and Jordan in 1732 and the stop list he gave differs somewhat from Bicknell's. Notably, Leffler mentioned a French Horn instead of a Cremona on the Great.

---

[18] Lonsdale, *Dr Charles Burney*, 23–4.

erecting an organ upon the theatre stage was 'undoubtedly to difference as much by its dignified form, as by its solemn tones, that semi-dramatic species of composition the Oratorio from a genuine Opera'.[19] The genre perfectly articulated the two conflicting demands of seriousness and elegant entertainment, which the members of polite society valued highly.[20] Other composers of organ concertos in the period capitalised on what Handel's organ concertos had initiated, and so did Burney. Thus, by performing his own organ concerto, Burney symbolically took the place of, and assumed the role of, Handel and Stanley. Thanks to this double appointment at St Dionis Backchurch and the King's Arms Tavern concerts, Burney rapidly acquired a good reputation as an organist. He appeared as a soloist in other public concerts and, consequently, his income increased substantially.

In 1751, however, he fell very ill and was confined to his bed for three months with severe fever. His physician, Dr John Armstrong, 'insisted that Burney leave the smoky atmosphere of London'[21] and consequently Burney and his family moved to King's Lynn in 1752, where, upon the death of John Barlow, the incumbent organist at St Margaret's, Burney was offered the post, thanks to the intercession of Sir John Turner, third Baronet and Member of Parliament for King's Lynn.[22] Burney was to stay there until 1760. The normal salary of £20 was increased by subscription to £100 (a substantial sum at the time), 'as an encouragem^t to a regular bred musician of some character to come down from the capital to instruct the children of the principal families in the town and Neighbourhood in Music'.[23] Burney initially found the organ of St Margaret's 'excecrably bad [*sic*]' and the local citizens crude and ignorant, as he reported in his *Memoirs* and wrote to his wife in a letter (*Letters*, 'To Mrs Burney', 30 September 1751). On Burney's advice and recommendation, the Swiss-born organ builder John Snetzler was entrusted with the construction of a new instrument at a cost of £700.[24] On 28 March 1754, the London *Evening Post* published the following announcement: 'Last Sunday the new Organ at King's Lynn, Norfolk, erected in St Margaret's Church by Mr. John Snetzler, of Oxford Road, was opened by Mr. Burney, and gave the utmost Satisfaction, being for

---

[19] William Mason, *Essays, Historical and Critical, on English Church Music* (York, 1795) republished in *The Works of William Mason* (London: T. Cadell and W. Davies, 1811), 72–3. See Pierre Dubois, 'Generic Hybridization of the Organ Voluntary, from Henry Purcell to William Russell', in *Palette pour Marie-Madeleine Martinet*, http://www.csti.paris-sorbonne.fr/centre/palette/txt/duboisMMMthesesHDR03.pdf, 2016.

[20] See Pierre Dubois, 'The Socio-Cultural Semiotics of Handel's Organ Concertos', *B. I. O. S. Journal*, no. 34 (2010), 68–81.

[21] Lonsdale, *Dr Charles Burney*, 36.　　[22] Lonsdale, *Dr Charles Burney*, 37.

[23] Quoted in Lonsdale, *Dr Charles Burney*, 37.

[24] Alan Barnes and Martin Renshaw, *The Life and Work of John Snetzler* (Aldershot: Scolar Press, 1994), 83.

Figure 3 The Snetzler organ in King's Lynn, in its current position © Pierre
Dubois

Sweetness of Tone and variety of Stops, universally esteemed one of the finest
Instruments in England.'[25]

The King's Lynn organ (see Figure 3) was important in Snetzler's career as
it established his reputation. It was his largest instrument (with twenty-seven
stops; Table 2). The Harris organ at St Dionis Backchurch, discussed above,
may have been a model for the King's Lynn instrument,[26] as the presence of
a French Horn, in particular, may suggest.[27] It had a 'Great Bourdon', which
was a novelty. Burney wrote that this 'borduun' is 'an octave below the Open
Diapason, and has the effect of a double bass in the chorus' (*History*, II,
345 n.). Another novelty was the Dulciana stop. The King's Lynn organ was
the first instrument into which this stop had been introduced in England.
According to Burney himself, Snetzler,

> a worthy man & excellent workman, had, during his Apprenticeship, worked at
> the celebrated Organ at Harlem, in Holland; and introduced several Stops into
> the Lynn Organ, from that renowned instrument, particularly the *Dulciana*
> stop, of wch the tone is extremely sweet & delicate. It is now introduced as

---

[25] Quoted in Scholes, *The Great Dr Burney*, 79.

[26] Barnes and Renshaw, *The Life and Work of John Snetzler*, 27, 280.

[27] Barnes and Renshaw, *The Life and Work of John Snetzler*, 258.

Table 2 King's Lynn: Stop list[*]

Great	Choir	Swell
Double Diapason to CC	Dulciana	Open Diapason
Open Diapason	Stop^d Diapason	Stop^d Diapason
Stop^d Diapason	Principal	Dulciana
Principal	Flute	German Flute to mid-C
Twelfth	Fifteenth	Cornet 4 ranks
Fifteenth	Bassoon to G above mid-C	French Horn
Tierce	Vox Humana	Trumpet
Sesquialtera V		Hautboy
Furniture VI		
Trumpet		
Clarion		
Cornet VII [*sic*] to C		

[*] From the 'Sperling Notebook', quoted in Boeringer, *Organa Britannica*, vol. II, 349. See also the *Leffler Manuscript*, 143.

a solo stop in all our best Chamber Organs, and has this advantage over the reed Stops, that is [*sic*] stands in tune as well as the open diapason, wth wch it is in unison. (*Memoirs*, 117)

The Dulciana consists of narrow-scaled, cylindrical pipes and it produces a very soft, delicate sound, not unlike that produced by a Salicional or a Viola da Gamba. That this particular stop was introduced in King's Lynn precisely at the time when Burney supervised the reconstruction of the organ is therefore a telling indication of the conception he had of the instrument, and of the importance he gave to a reserved, moderate volume of sound, as opposed to excessive power or 'noise', as we shall see below. On the Snetzler organ at King's Lynn, the Dulciana had a full compass down to G', so that it was conceived as a 'suitable accompanimental stop', and 'in this Burney was well ahead of his time, for this use of a Dulciana instead of an Open Diapason in a church organ was not revived until towards the end of the century'.[28]

The probable recommendation of Snetzler reveals Burney's readiness to embrace novelty. With its bright chorus, its numerous reed stops, its swell that included various solo reed stops and a German Flute and its two newly intro-duced Dulciana stops, the softness of which was generally admired, the King's

---

[28] Barnes and Renshaw, *The Life and Work of John Snetzler*, 27.

Lynn organ (Figure 3) offered all the palette of sonorities of which a mid-century English organist could dream.

In 1760, Burney and his family (he now had six children) finally managed to return to London. While his health had been restored, his wife's deteriorated and she died in 1762. In 1768, Burney was appointed organist of the Oxford Chapel, Marylebone, later called St Peter's (after 1832), in Vere Street.[29] The chapel was built by Edward Harley, second Earl of Oxford, was designed by James Gibbs in 1722 and opened in 1724. It was originally intended as a Chapel of Ease to supplement All Souls, Langham Place, in the parish of Marylebone, as the population increased and the old church proved insufficient to receive all the parishioners.

The contract for the organ, signed by Christopher Schrider in 1722,[30] was submitted to the approval of Dr William Croft, organist of Westminster Abbey, and John Weldon, organist of the Chapel Royal. Christopher Schrider may have worked with Abraham Jordan.[31]

> The Great Organ to contain the Open Diapason of metal in the front from C in alt' down to gamut, & the rest to answer by communication with the Stop Diapason or without and the base and the treble to be agreeable to the ear. The stop to contain 49 pipes. The Stop Diapason of wood & to contain 49 pipes. The Principal of metal & to contain 49 pipes. The Cornet of 3 ranks of metal 72 pipes. A Trumpet stop throughout with metal 49 pipes. The Fifteenth of metal 49 pipes.
>
> The Chair Organ to have the Stop Diapason of 49 pipes. A flute stop of wood 49 pipes. A Cremona stop & to contain 49 pipes.[32]

The instrument (Table 3) was apparently completed in 1724. As the contract shows, the organ was a small instrument with two manuals and a short compass of only forty-nine notes, which cost £300. It remained unaltered until 1852.

Compared to the Snetzler organ that Burney had played at St Margaret's, King's Lynn, the Oxford chapel instrument must have appeared somewhat limited. Ever concerned about social prestige and respectability, however, Burney certainly found the position interesting for its possible associations and the musical reputation of the chapel. The famous composer William Boyce had been the chapel's organist from 1734 to 1736, and it is interesting to note that this is generally assumed to be the very chapel whose interior is represented in

---

[29] Donovan Dawe remarks that the long-accepted date of 1763 for Burney's appointment to the Oxford Chapel is wrong and should in reality be 1768. Dawe, *The Organists of the City of London*, 85.

[30] Quoted in Colin Goulden, *The Organs of All Souls Church, Langham Place, London, and St Peter's Church, Vere Street, London* (London: All Soul's Church, 1976), 12.

[31] Boeringer, *Organa Britannica*, vol. II, 311.

[32] Quoted in Goulden, *The Organs of All Souls Church*, 12.

Table 3 Oxford Chapel, Marylebone: Stop list[*]

Great	Choir
Open Diapason	Stop^d Diapason
Stop^d Diapason	Flute
Principal	Cremona
Fifteenth	
Trumpet	
Cornet III	

[*] Boeringer, *Organa Britannica*, vol. II, 311. See also the *Leffler Manuscript*, 80.

plate 2 of William Hogarth's print series *Industry and Idleness* (1747), 'The Industrious 'Prentice Performing the Duty of a Christian' (see Figure 4), and possibly also in the 'marriage scene' (plate 5) of *A Rake's Progress* (1734).[33]

In Hogarth's engraving, the congregation appears to be a very large one, gathered around the organ in the loft that acts as the focal point of the picture. Small as it was, a crucial role is thus symbolically conferred upon the organ by Hogarth: that of being the centre around which the congregation and choir gather together in worship and singing (here, 'O How I Love Thy Law', Psalm CXIX, Verse 97, inscribed underneath the picture). The very presence of an organ indicates the wealth and respectability of the church, while the great number of people (probably exaggerated visually by the artist) and the assiduous attitude of the good apprentice suggest that this was a notable place of worship, something to which Burney must have been sensitive.

Finally, in 1783, having failed to get appointed organist at St Martin-in-the-Fields as successor to Joseph Kelway,[34] Burney was appointed organist of the Royal Hospital Chelsea, an institution founded by Charles II to provide accommodation and care for veterans of the British army. There was initially no organ at the Royal Hospital but, shortly after the establishment opened in 1692, Captain Matthew Ingram, the first Major and Lieutenant Governor, presented an organ made by Renatus Harris, the case of which is still extant today (see Figure 5). This led to an organist being appointed, at a salary of £20 per annum,[35] but without apartments, as all the accommodation had already been allocated to other members

---

[33] John Gorton, *A Topographical Dictionary of Great Britain and Ireland* (London: Chapman and Hall, 1833), II, 778; John Timbs, *Curiosities of London* (London: David Rogue, 1867), 183.

[34] Lonsdale, *Dr Charles Burney*, 295.

[35] See Royal Hospital Accounts reproduced in Dan Cruikshank, *The Royal Hospital Chelsea – the Place and the People* (London: Third Millennium Publishing, 2004), 66–7.

Figure 4 William Hogarth, 'The Industrious 'Prentice Performing the Duty of a Christian', *Industry and Idleness*, plate 2 (1747)

Figure 5 The Organ at the Royal Hospital Chelsea, © William Vann, Organist and Director of Music, Royal Hospital Chelsea (2020)

of the staff.[36] Burney owed his nomination to Edmund Burke, as his last act of office as Paymaster General in the Fox–North Coalition.[37] 'One day, after dinner at Sir Joshua Reynolds', Frances Burney (Mme D'Arblay, Burney's daughter) reported,

> Mr Burke drew Dr Burney aside and with great delicacy, and feeling his way, by the most investigating looks, as he proceeded, said that the organist's place at Chelsea College was then vacant: that it was but twenty pounds a year, but that, to a man of Dr Burney's eminence, if it should be worth his acceptance, it might be raised to fifty.[38]

Burney accepted the offer. There were two services in the chapel per day, but most were performed by a deputy, to whom Burney paid £10 a year, while he would play for the Sunday morning services.[39] The diarist John Marsh (1752–1828), an amateur musician and composer who was assistant organist at Chichester Cathedral, reported in his *Journals* that in 1798, happening to spend the day at Chelsea with his brother Henry, he went to the chapel, where he was introduced to Mr Bach, 'deputy organist to Dr Burney', so that he (Marsh) 'sat in the organ loft & played one of [his] trumpet pieces for the voluntary after the Psalms, w'ch was the only one played there, there never being any after service of an afternoon'.[40] This suggests that the deputy had only a limited role and confined himself to performing minimal duties. The same Bach gave up the organ to Marsh on another similar occasion, in June 1802, as 'Dr Burney now very seldom, it seem'd attended himself'.[41] Burney was now seventy-six years old and did not play very often.

From the *Memoirs* completed by Frances Burney, it appears that, at the time of his appointment in 1783, Burney wished 'for some retreat from, yet near London',[42] and that he hoped to be accommodated in the College. Yet he had to continue to live at his house in St Martin's Street until June 1788, if not later, the Chelsea apartment being vacated only after the death of the Rev. William Jennings, the First Chaplain, in the autumn of 1787.[43] The plan of Burney's apartments (as shown in a sketch published by C. G. T. Dean, Captain of the

---

[36] Captain C. G. T. Dean, 'Dr Burney's Connection with the Royal Hospital, Chelsea', *Transactions of the London and Middlesex Archaeological Society*, new series, vol. IX (London: Bishopsgate Institute, 1948), 11.

[37] Frances Burney [Mme D'Arblay], *Memoirs of Dr Burney* (London: Edward Moxon, 1832), vol. II, 376.

[38] Frances Burney, *Memoirs of Dr Burney*, vol. II, 373.   [39] Lonsdale, *Dr Charles Burney*, 296.

[40] John Marsh, 'History of my private Life', *The John Marsh Journals*, ed. Brian Robins (Stuyvesant, NY: Pendragon Press, 1998), 664. From 1805, Burney's deputy was Charles Edward Horn. See Michael Kassler, *The English Translations of Forkel's Life of Bach*, in *The English Bach Awakening*, ed. Michael Kassler (Abingdon: Ashgate Publishing/Routledge, 2004/2016), 169–210, 177.

[41] Marsh, 'History of my private life', 737.

[42] Frances Burney, *Memoirs of Dr Burney*, vol. II, 374.

[43] Dean, 'Dr Burney's Connection', 12.

Invalids, in an article from 1948),[44] where Frances Burney lived with her father until her marriage to the French exile General Alexandre D'Arblay in 1793,[45] shows its proximity to the chapel.

Burney's appointment at the Royal Hospital was 'of small pecuniary value, [yet] it would have been esteemed on account of its associations',[46] as it enabled Burney to rub shoulders with numerous prominent men, such as the Governors and Lieutenant Governors, architects Samuel Wyatt and John Soane and surgeons Robin Adair and Thomas Keate, who attended George III during his temporary insanity. In 1798, however, Burney had to relinquish his apartments to the Rev. William Haggitt, who had been promoted to First Chaplain, and he moved upstairs to the Second Chaplain's flat on the second floor, where he was to stay until his death on 12 April 1814.[47] Both Burney and his daughter Frances were eventually to be buried in the burial ground of the Royal Hospital.

Thanks to his social connections and musical reputation, Burney certainly contributed to increasing the lustre of the Royal Hospital, as eminent people would visit and attend services in the chapel.[48] Notably, it was in his apartments at Chelsea College that he was to welcome Joseph Haydn during the composer's two major London visits (1791–1792 and 1794–1795). In May 1791, Burney arranged a small musical party at Chelsea College with Haydn, and Thomas Twining and other friends played Haydn's *Seven Last Words of Christ* together.[49] Besides, the chapel was used on important occasions, such as the service of thanksgiving for George III's recovery from his bout of insanity in 1789.[50]

The original organ erected in the Chapel by Renatus Harris in 1695 was probably altered by Jordan in 1715, and subsequently maintained by Renatus Harris and Gerard Smith.[51] It was not very large, as it contained only nineteen stops on three manuals (Table 4). Burney was succeeded by Charles Wesley (from 1814 to 1817) and an organ by Gray installed in 1822. The current instrument is by Hill, Norman & Beard, in the original Harris case.

What is striking in Burney's four appointments as an organist is the social prestige attached to the posts he held. He may not always have had very large instruments at his disposal, but the churches for which he worked were all elegant and polite ones, situated in wealthy, respectable areas. The organs he knew and played were typical English organs of the period and must have

---

[44]   Dean, 'Dr Burney's Connection', 14.
[45]   See www.chelsea-pensioners.co.uk/music-music-lists.
[46]   Dean, 'Dr Burney's Connection', 15.   [47] Dean, 'Dr Burney's Connection', 15–16.
[48]   Cruikshank, *The Royal Hospital Chelsea*, 90.   [49] Lonsdale, *Dr Charles Burney*, 355.
[50]   *London Evening Post*, 14 March 1789, quoted in Cruikshank, *The Royal Hospital Chelsea*, 92.
[51]   See Boeringer, *Organa Britannica*, vol. II, 248–9.

Table 4 Royal Hospital Chelsea: Stop list[*]

Great	Choir	Swell
Open Diapason	Stop^d Diapason	Open Diapason
Open Diapason	Principal	Stop^d Diapason
Stop^d Diapason	Flute	Principal
Principal	Fifteenth	Cornet III
Twelfth		Trumpet
Fifteenth		Hautboy
Sesquialtera V		
Trumpet		
Cornet V		

[*] From the 'Sperling Notebook', quoted in Boeringer, *Organa Britannica*, vol. II, 248.

greatly contributed to the making of his own taste and aesthetic preferences. In the *Cyclopedia*, he was to sum up the qualities he thought necessary in a good organ: it should have 'a good stopped diapason, as that stop is the foundation of the organ', so this should 'be sufficiently bold in the base';

> no stop should be loudest at the top. Of the open diapason, little more need be said than that it should be full, smooth, and articulate. ... As a single stop should not be loudest at the top, so the chorus should not predominate over the diapasons ... the chorus should be rich, brilliant, and articulate; and the twelfth and tierce, and their octaves, should not be heard, except when listened for. The trumpet-stop, when good, adds greatly to the majesty, as well as to the strength of the chorus ... And it had been well if the trumpet had never been used as any other than a chorus-stop .... (*Cyclopedia*, vol. 25, n.p.)

Burney's insistence on roundness of tone, smoothness, a brilliant and majestic chorus, no loud stop predominating at the top, and his recommendation of not using the trumpet as a solo stop, indicate that he expected the organ to be both bold and round in the base but restrained in the treble. The organ must not shout or scream, but be of moderate power. It must be bright and full of majesty, but not too loud, and he liked soft stops such as the Dulciana. The balance to be aimed for was that of a perfect dialectics of moderation and sublimity, quite at one with the English ethical and aesthetics ideals of the age (see Section 3 below).[52]

In 1786, on the death of John Stanley who had been Master of the King's Band since the death of William Boyce in 1779, Burney had great expectations

---

[52] See Pierre Dubois, *L'orgue dans la société anglaise au XVIIIème siècle: éthique et esthétique de la modération* (Lille: Presses Universitaires du Septentrion, 1997), *passim*.

to be appointed in Stanley's place, which indicates that he was one of the foremost organists of the time. Unfortunately for him, William Parsons was chosen by Lord Salisbury, the Lord Chamberlain, to Burney's great disappointment. The fact that the satirist John Wolcot mentioned Burney's failure to obtain the post in his *Ode Upon Ode* (signed 'Peter Pindar')[53] shows that the competition had been a subject of public interest, as Roger Lonsdale noted.[54] The King himself was displeased with the appointment of Parsons by Salisbury, as he remarked to Frances Burney.[55]

In 1784, Burney was appointed official historian of the great Handel Commemoration (and had therefore to interrupt the writing of the third volume of his *History*). In 1801, he undertook the writing of the music articles for Rees's *Cyclopedia*, which occupied him for much of the rest of his life. However, as we have seen, his love of the organ never flagged.

2 Burney's Pieces for the Organ

Charles Burney's catalogue of compositions was relatively modest. It may be surmised that, like most composers of his time, his greatest ambition would probably have been to compose operas. It is revealing that, in his *History of Music*, he should have devoted so many pages (over 300 in the original edition) to 'Italian Opera in England' (Chapter VI of Book IV). Opera was considered as the ultimate genre because it effected the fusion (or marriage) of music and poetry, and it was the most lavish and spectacular form of entertainment. It encapsulated the musical and theatrical ideals of the age, and was the locus of social and ideological representations, attended as it was by the gentility and upper classes.

Burney's attempts to compose for the stage were, however, thwarted. His literary pursuits – and especially the writing of the *History of Music*, which kept him busy for about twenty years – prevented him from devoting enough time and energy to music proper. His only real theatrical success was his own translation and adaptation of Jean-Jacques Rousseau's *Le devin du village* under the title of *The Cunning Man* (1766–67). Apart from this, a few anthems, a few songs for the masques *Alfred* and *Queen Mab* in the 1750s, his *Canzonetti a due voci in canone* on poetry by Metastasio (*c.*1790) and the composition for chorus, soloist and orchestra, *I will love thee, O Lord my strength* (Ps xviii), which he submitted as a DMus exercise in Oxford in 1769, most of his other compositions consist of instrumental chamber music: six lessons for the

[53] John Wolcot, *Ode Upon Ode* (London: G. Kearsley and W. Forster, 1787), 38–9.
[54] Lonsdale, *Dr Charles Burney*, 320–1.
[55] Frances Burney, *Memoirs of Dr Burney*, vol. III, 78–9.

harpsichord, six sonatas for the harpsichord or piano, two sets of sonatas for the harpsichord or piano with accompaniments for violin and violoncello, sonatas for two violins and a bass, six duets for two German flutes, three concertos for the harpsichord and six concertos for the violin in eight parts. One of his best-known works is his Four Sonatas or Duets for two Performers on one Piano Forte or Harpsichord, composed in 1777. It is probable that other compositions by Burney remained in manuscript form and were never published. We saw above that he composed an organ concerto for his first concert at the King's Arms Tavern and he may have composed others, yet none have so far come to light.

However, apart from these works of instrumental and chamber music, Burney published two sets of music for the organ. The first one is a set of Cornet pieces entitled *Six Cornet Pieces with an introduction for the Diapasons and a Fugue for the organ*, composed early in 1751 and published by Walsh in London around 1760 (see Figure 6). The second one is entitled *Preludes, Fugues, and Interludes; for the Organ. Alphabetically arranged in all the keys that are most perfectly in tune upon that Instrument & printed in a Pocket size for the convenience of Young Organists, for whose use this book is particularly calcu-lated & Published by Chas. Burney, Mus. D.* It is one of Burney's latest works, composed around 1787. Only the first volume of this second set seems to have been published. The fact that these organs works were composed respectively at the beginning and at the end of Burney's career shows a lasting interest in, and true dedication to, the organ. They may not be demanding or ambitious works, but they are characteristic of the dominant idiom of the eighteenth-century English organ voluntary. As Francis Routh noted about the *Six Cornet Pieces*, Burney's 'Voluntaries [*sic*] continue fairly and squarely in the mainstream of his predecessors. His style is straightforward, and the Handel influence is particu-larly marked; the right-hand part is chiefly melodic, while the secondary left hand provides the harmonic background.'[56] Quite in harmony with the English practice of the time, Burney's organ pieces never call for the use of pedals. Indications of registrations are almost non-existent: 'Diapasons' is mentioned for the prelude of the first set of pieces, while all the other six pieces of the same set are clearly specified to be for the Cornet, which places them within a distinct genre in English eighteenth-century organ music. There is no mention of registration at all in the second set of pieces. Unlike Stanley or Russell, who both gave precise indications concerning the registrations to be used in each voluntary, Burney does not appear to have been a colourist and he must have

---

[56] Francis Routh, *Early English Organ Music* (New York: Harper & Row Publishers, Inc., 1973), 203.

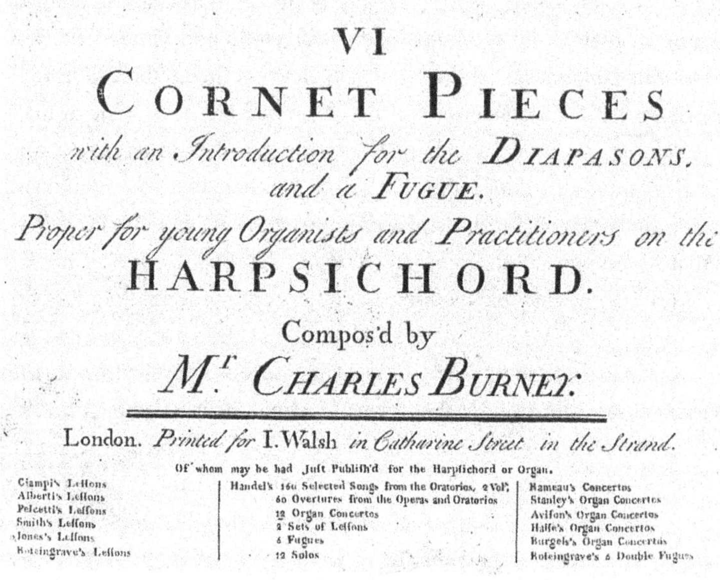

VI
CORNET PIECES
with an Introduction for the DIAPASONS,
and a FUGUE.
Proper for young Organists and Practitioners on the
HARPSICHORD.
Compos'd by
Mr. CHARLES BURNEY.

London. Printed for I. Walsh in Catharine Street in the Strand.

Of whom may be had Just Publish'd for the Harpsichord or Organ.

Ciampi's Lessons
Alberti's Lessons
Pelcetti's Lessons
Smith's Lessons
Jones's Lessons
Roseingrave's Lessons

Handel's 160 Selected Songs from the Oratorios, 2 Vol.
60 Overtures from the Operas and Oratorios
12 Organ Concertos
2 Sets of Lessons
6 Fugues
12 Solos

Rameau's Concertos
Stanley's Organ Concertos
Avison's Organ Concertos
Hasse's Organ Concertos
Burgess's Organ Concertos
Roseingrave's 6 Double Fugues

Figure 6 Charles Burney, title page, *Six Cornet Pieces*, *c.*1760

assumed that organists would naturally resort to the standard registrations used at the time.

The first piece of the first set is an 'Introduction' (or rather: 'Introduzzione', as Burney wrote) for the Diapasons (see Figure 7). It is followed by the six Cornet pieces and concluded by a fugue. In the eighteenth century, it was common for the voluntary (when, as was usual, it consisted of two or more distinct movements) to open on a slow movement for the Diapasons, which was supposed to create a calm atmosphere of religious meditation, while the following movement (e.g. on the Cornet) provided a contrast with its brisk and lively character. In his *History of Music*, John Hawkins described the way Handel preluded his organ concertos:

> When he gave a concerto, his method in general was to introduce it with a voluntary movement on the diapasons, which stole on the ear in a slow and solemn progression; the harmony close wrought, and as full as could possibly be expressed; the passages concatenated with stupendous art, the whole at the same time being perfectly intelligible, and carrying the appearance of great simplicity. This kind of prelude was succeeded by the concerto itself, which he executed with a degree of spirit and firmness that no one ever pretended to equal.[57]

[57] John Hawkins, *A General History of the Science and Practice of Music* (London, 1776, republished: London: Novello, 1875), vol. II, 912.

Figure 7 Charles Burney, 'Introduzzione', *Six Cornet Pieces*, c.1760, p. 1

The slow Diapason introduction to Handel's concertos described by Hawkins was manifestly borrowed from the practice of the voluntary. In several sermons, the voluntary was defined by two complementary, almost contradictory, functions: on the one hand, to 'assuage the temper', and on the other to enliven the spirit and shake the congregation out of its lethargy, as many authors of sermons stressed.[58] George Coningesby wrote that men still had 'the same Affections to be composed when irregular, and when dull to be enliven'd; our Devotion is at least as flat and languid as ever, and our Attention as easily withdrawn'.[59] Richard Banner insisted on the necessity of instilling calm and moderation so as to check men's 'unruly passions' and channel them towards 'Extacies of heavenly Joy': 'Are our Minds then enraged with Passion, and transported with heat, It [Music] can infuse into them such a grave, sedate, and sober Mediocrity, as not only to allay those exhorbitant sallies, but to change our unruly Passions into more exalted Extacies of heavenly Joy.'[60] Interestingly, the two-pronged function ascribed to church music amounts to a definition of the balanced opposites that make up the aesthetic of the English organ, both refined and elevated, calm and serene. It implies balance, moderation and an almost

[58] See Pierre Dubois, 'The Organ and its Music Vindicated' – a Study of "Music Sermons" in Eighteenth-Century England', *B.I.O.S. Journal*, no. 31 (2007), 40–64.

[59] George Coningesby, *Church Music Vindicated; and the Causes of its Dislikes Enquired into* (London, 1733), 15.

[60] Richard Banner, *The Use and Antiquity of Musick in the Services of God* (Oxford, 1737), 19.

impossible but ideal state of perfect equilibrium between activity or energy on the one hand, and stasis and tranquillity on the other.

What is slightly unusual in Burney's arrangement of pieces in the first set is that only one slow Diapason movement is prefixed to the whole, instead of one for each piece, which would have created a conventional, regular, systematic binary opposition between slow and fast movements in each chosen key. Burney's Diapason movement is clearly not intended to be used as an introduction to every Cornet piece, but rather as an introduction to the book as a whole, or simply to the first Cornet piece, which is in the same key. Conversely, this movement may be seen as a model for improvising similar harmonic sequences and textures as preludes to the other Cornet movements in other keys and to the final fugue. Similarly, the Fugue is a conclusion to the whole set rather than to any particular piece, as none of the Cornet pieces are in F minor. The conventional structure of the voluntary is thus disrupted. The keys used are as follows:

1. Introduzzione (Diapasons): E minor
2. Cornet Piece No. I: E minor
3. Cornet Piece No. II: A major
4. Cornet Piece No. III: D major
5. Cornet Piece No. IV: B minor
6. Cornet Piece No. V: E flat major
7. Cornet Piece No. VI: B flat major
8. Fugue: F minor

Peter Williams remarked that 'for the solo stops, Stanley's [voluntaries] were the model'.[61] While Stanley's voluntaries, when composed, were relatively 'modern', being in the contemporary instrumental style of Corelli, Vivaldi and Handel, the voluntary became conservative in its stylistic stability, as composers retained the formula made popular by Stanley.[62] As for the Cornet voluntary, it became gradually less popular, as it was often criticised for its lightness or levity.[63] John Marsh wrote:

> For the Cornet, quick Music, in a brilliant style, without double notes or chords, is proper. This Stop, though frequently used in Voluntaries before the first Lesson, is yet, I think, of too light and airy a nature for the Church: I would therefore recommend it's [*sic*] being used but sparingly in

[61] Peter Williams, 'Preface' to *Twelve Voluntaries for Organ or Harpsichord by William Boyce or Maurice Green* (London: Galliard Limited, 1969), ii.

[62] Brian William Luckner, 'The Organ Voluntaries of John Stanley', Doctoral thesis, University of Cincinnati, 1992 (reproduced by University Microfilms International, Ann Arbor, MI), 103.

[63] See John L. Speller, 'Before the First Lesson: A Study of Some Eighteenth-Century Voluntaries in Relation to the Instruments on Which They Were Played', *B.I.O.S. Journal*, no. 20 (1996), 64–84, 73, 79.

Voluntaries, and only in the Minor key, except on Festivals or joyful occasions, for which it may properly be reserved.[64]

However, Burney resolutely persevered in writing Cornet voluntaries at the beginning of his career, and not only in the minor mode! His definition of music at the beginning of his *History of Music* as an 'innocent luxury, unnecessary, indeed, to our existence, but a great improvement and gratification of the sense of hearing' (*History*, I, 21) finds an illustration in his choice of the Cornet voluntary for his first set of organ compositions. Music, he wrote elsewhere, is 'the art of pleasing by the succession and combination of agreeable sounds' (*History*, II, 7). He obviously did not intend to write in a serious polyphonic style. His Cornet voluntaries are not deep or solemn pieces, and they may have been intended for private practice on chamber organs rather than for the Church. Their essentially melodic character is reminiscent of light baroque concertos in the Italian manner and close in character and spirit to the Cornet voluntaries of William Walond, the Oxford organist and composer. As for the fugue in F minor which concludes the set, it shows the influence of Handel, as its theme and its motif of three repeated notes in the countersubject are reminiscent of Handel's first Fugue in G Minor from *Six Fugues or Voluntaries*, published by Walsh in 1735.

Scholes remarked that 'what strikes one in both [organ] books [by Burney] is the failure to appreciate the essential difference between organ style and harpsichord style. Both books include passages that are plainly harpsichord music.'[65] However, some remarks by Burney seem to give the lie to this assertion. After hearing Mr Pothoff, the organist of the Old Church in Amsterdam (see Section 5) play the organ, Burney noted that Pothoff was a harpsichord player, but that he was 'so well acquainted with the different genius of the organ, that his most rapid flights ... occasioned none of those unpleasing vacuities of sound, which so commonly happen, when this instrument is touched by a *mere* harpsichord player' (*Music in Germany*, II, 289). In his *History of Music*, Burney remarked that 'Frescobaldi introduced a superior style of treating the organ, divested of rapid and frivolous divisions, which disgrace that most noble and comprehensive of all instruments' (*History*, II, 98). In Rome, Burney visited the largest instrument, a thirty-two-foot organ with thirty-six stops on two manuals and pedals. He remarked that the organist, Signor Colista, was 'very dextrous' on the pedals and that he played in 'the true organ style, though his taste [was] rather ancient', adding that 'the organ stile

---

[64] John Marsh, 'Preface', *Eighteen Voluntaries for the Organ, Chiefly intended for the Use of Young Practitioners* (London: Preston, 1791), vi.

[65] Scholes, *The Great Dr Burney*, I, 61.

seems better preserved throughout Italy as it is with us' because the harpsichord is less cultivated than in England. One of the Dominicans at the Jesuits' church plays 'with a very uncommon brilliancy of execution' albeit in 'a stile of playing more suitable to the harpsichord than organ, but, in its way ... very masterly and powerful' (*Music in France*, 17). Thus, Burney was obviously well acquainted with the difference between the respective styles of each instrument but deliberately intended his pieces to be playable on both, as the subtitle of the *Cornet Pieces* makes clear: 'Proper for Young Organists and Practitioners on the harpsichord.'

Indeed, his description of Armand-Louis Couperin's organ style (at St-Gervais, Paris) confirms Burney's attention to the proper character and touch required for the instrument. He considered that harpsichord passages could be integrated in a performance on the organ, provided this was done appropriately:

> Great latitude is allowed to the performer in these interludes; nothing is too light or too grave, all styles are admitted, and though M. Couperin has the true organ touch, smooth and connected: yet he often tried, and not unsuccessfully, mere harpsichord passages, smartly articulated, and the notes detached and separated. (*Music in France*, 42)

Andrew McRea sums up well the character of Burney's Cornet pieces:

> Burney's movements do not really measure up to the intuitive, fluent, and well-controlled movements of Stanley, but they do reveal skill in coining thematic material appropriate to key, deploying figuration (even if it is rather saturated by sequence which is not always contrapuntally strong in conception), and in the handling of form according to the ritornello principle.[66]

Burney's second volume, which may be a little more ambitious than the first, follows a different kind of structure: the pieces are all in two parts – a slow introduction or prelude, followed by a fugue, with a few 'interludes' (as mentioned in the title) inserted between (Figures 8 and 9). These consist in 'fughettas' (and one fugue) interspersed at random between the introductions and fugues. Here, below, is the order, keys and movements of the pieces:

1. Introduction (andante) and fuga (allegro) in A minor.
2. Interlude: fughetta in A minor.
3. Introduction (grave) and fuga (allegro) in A minor.
4. Introduction (andante) and fuga (alla breve) in A major.
5. Interlude: fughetta in A major.
6. Introduction (moderato) and fuga (allegro) in A major.

---

[66] Andrew McCrea, 'Introduction', *Charles Burney Six Cornet Pieces* (Stratford-upon-Avon: Royal College of Organists, March 2015), 5.

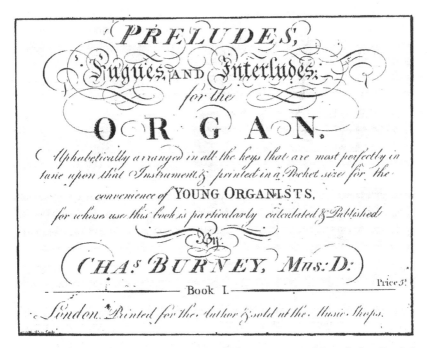

Figure 8 Charles Burney, title page, *Preludes, Fugues and Interludes*, Book I, 1787

Figure 9 Charles Burney, 'Introduction', *Preludes, Fugues and Interludes*, Book I, 1787, p. 1

7. Introduction (andante) and fuga (allegro) in B flat major.
8. Fuga (allegro) in B flat major.
9. Andante and fuga (allegro) in B flat major.
10. Introduction (allegretto) and fuga in C major.
11. Introduction (adagio) and fughetta (allegro) in C major.
12. Untitled fuga in C major.
13. Grave and fuga (allegro) in C minor.
14. Introduction (maestosa [*sic*]) and fuga (allegro) in D major.

The organisation of the volume is somewhat lopsided. Burney is not very consistent, since No. 8 is yet another fugue in the same key as the 'Prelude and fugue' that precedes it. Nos. 9 and 13 do not bear the title 'introduction' like the others preceding, and No. 12 is designated as a fugue and not presented as an 'interlude'.

Burney's intention seems to have been to write 'serious' music for the keyboard, following the model set by Thomas Roseingrave's *Six Double Fugues for the Organ or Harpsichord* and Handel's *Six Fugues or Voluntarys*. However, the style is different, both from these models and from Burney's earlier set of Cornet pieces. Burney had by now adopted the *galant* mode and there are also forays into expressive chromaticism (see Fugue No. 2 in A Minor for instance), dramatic passages (see No. 7, Introduction in B Flat Major) and sudden modulations. As we shall see below, Burney admired organists who played in a grave and 'masterly' manner, which he deemed to be 'the true style' of church music, so he may have intended to show his ability to compose serious material, while allowing space for lighter passages so as to avoid the effect of 'laboured contrivances' that he denounced in his criticism of some German music.

The counterpoint never ventures beyond three real parts, however, even though there may be some 'filling in', and, as was common, the fugues are hardly regular and certainly less elaborate and complex than the German model. At times, Burney breaks the discourse with sudden flights of agile figurations in semiquavers (see end of the Fughetta in A Minor, No. 2, or the last Fugue in B Flat, No. 9). While the dotted rhythm in the 2nd Introduction in A minor, No. 3, may remind us of the standard Handelian overtures in the French style, other movements belong to a more modern, graceful idiom (see for example the Andante in B Flat, No. 9, the 1st Introduction in C, No. 10 and the 2nd Fugue in C, No. 12; see Figure 10). The left hand occasionally lapses into simple Alberti bass accompaniment figurations and arpeggios in the *galant* manner, as for instance in the 1st Fugue in C, No. 10. The texture is sometimes amplified by octaves and chords, and Burney also resorts to parallel octaves or unisons in the classical orchestral manner (see Andante in B Flat, No. 9, or the end of the Fugues in C, No. 10 and No. 12).

Figure 10 Charles Burney, second page of Fugue in C, No. 12, *Preludes, Fugues and Interludes*, Book I, 1787

Burney makes full use of the then-common long GG compass of the manuals to increase the effect in the bass and create an impression of gravitas and solemnity (see for instance 'Introduction', p. 1, bars 1–4 and 20–23, and concluding bars of several other movements). The fugues often evince rhythmic dynamism and energy and may call to mind some of William Russell's organ fugues, although these are generally more developed than Burney's. Like his literary writing, Burney's music is direct, optimistic and energetic.

Even if Burney was, in later life, to denounce his own compositions as 'negligible', having devoted most of his energies to writing *about* music rather than to pursuing the career of practising musician and composer, there is ample evidence that he was a well-trained and able organist. He adhered to the English style of organ music and his pieces are perfectly suited to the English organ of the period. Interestingly, in the 'organ' entry in Rees's *Cyclopedia*, Burney included a cross-section (Figure 11; drawn by John Farey) of a typical eighteenth-century *English* organ, which shows his full adherence to this model of organ building:

Like the majority of published organ voluntaries in the eighteenth century, Burney's pieces are technically undemanding by modern standards. This

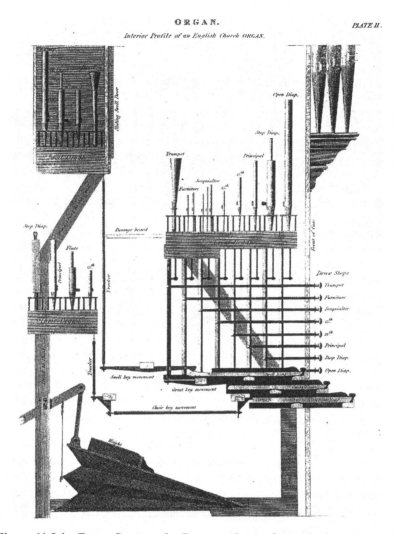

Figure 11 John Farey, *Section of a Georgian Organ*, from Abraham Rees, ed. *The Cyclopedia*, vol. 25, 1811

was a necessary condition for them to sell well and it explains why they were advertised as 'convenient for young organists'. But beyond this practical consideration, the technical simplicity and directness of Burney's pieces for the organ are at one with a musical ethos that eschews gratuitous complexity or pedantic sophistication, an ethos that is amply asserted in Burney's writings. This ethos was deeply rooted in the dominant philosophical and aesthetic conceptions of eighteenth-century Britain, to which we must now turn.

3 Historical and Ideological Context

A quick survey of European organs in the late-seventeenth and eighteenth centuries shows that the styles adopted in different countries varied enormously. These differences in style manifested themselves across a range of parameters – stop list, voicing, console-design, pedals, and so on – and had a direct link, naturally, with the contemporaneous repertoire performed on these various types of instruments, as well as national liturgical constraints within which the organ was used. These differences in style reflected markedly diverging aesthetic stances corresponding to deeply rooted philosophical, ideological, moral and social criteria. In both his organ compositions and his written observations about organs and organ music, Burney expressed an implicit theoretical aesthetic rationale that was grounded in the dominant contemporary discourse on taste and beauty, which must now be examined.

The history of the eighteenth-century organ actually began at the Restoration in 1660. During the Commonwealth, organs had been banned from religious services by the Puritans. The Lords and Commons Ordinance of 9 May 1644 ordered the 'speedy demolisshing of all organs, images and all matters of superstitious monuments in all Cathedralls, and Collegiate or Parish-Churches and Chapels throughout the kingdom of England'. It stipulated:

> The Lords and Commons assembled in Parliament, the better to accomplish the blessed Reformation so happily begun, and to remove all offences and things illegal in the worship of God, do Ordain, That all Representations of any of the Persons of the Trinity, or of any Angel or Saint, in or about any Cathedral, Collegiate or Parish Church, or Chappel, or in any open place within this Kingdome, shall be taken away, defaced, and utterly demolished ... And that all Organs, and the Frames or Cases wherein they stand in all Churches or Chappels aforesaid, shall be taken away, and utterly defaced, and none other hereafter set up in their places.[67]

For the Puritans, instrumental music was a Popish survival that was not compatible with the true form of religious practice they endeavoured to impose. They feared the congregation's attention might be distracted from the Word of God by instrumental music.[68] As a consequence, no pre-Commonwealth organ has survived complete. Only a few cases bear witness to the style and art of organ builders between the Reformation and the Restoration, such as St Stephen, Old Radnor (*c.* 1500–50), St Michael, Framlingham (*c.*1630),

---

[67] 'May 1644: An Ordinance for the further demolishing of Monuments of Idolatry and Superstition', in *Acts and Ordinances of the Interregnum, 1642–1660*, ed. C. H. Firth and R. S. Rait (London, 1911), 425–6.www.british-history.ac.uk/no-series/acts-ordinances-interregnum.

[68] See Hawkins, *A General History of the Science and Practice of Music*, II, 576–7.

Tewkesbury Abbey, Gloucestershire, and St Nicholas, Stanford-on-Avon (*c*.1632), the two last-mentioned being constituent parts of the organ formerly built by Robert Dallam for Magdalen College, Oxford. The discovery of two old soundboards at Wetheringsett, Suffolk (*c*.1520), in 1977, and Wingfield, Suffolk (undated), in 1995, made it possible (notably thanks to the Early English Organ Project) for organ builders Dominic Gwynn and the late Martin Goetze to attempt a reconstruction of the stop list and to build speculative copies of what a Reformation organ may have sounded like.[69]

After it had been excluded from religious services by the Puritans during the Commonwealth, the organ soon found its place again in the Anglican liturgy at the Restoration. It is worth noting however that this applied mainly to London and the large provincial towns and cities. In ordinary parish churches, the organ was a rarity, as it had been before the Commonwealth. Even in London, only 30 per cent of the churches possessed an organ by 1700, and the proportion was still less than 50 per cent by 1730.[70] Large market towns in the provinces acquired organs only gradually in the course of the eighteenth century. However, the instruments that had escaped destruction were repaired, and new organs were built. Organ builders, some of whom had worked before the Commonwealth and had been forced to stop their activity or even go abroad, resurfaced and resumed their trade: John Loosemore (Salisbury and Exeter, 1665), John and Robert Hayward (Wimborne Minster, 1664), Thomas Thamar (Winchester, 1665–70, Peterborough, 1661 and 1680), Lancelot Pease (Canterbury, 1662) and Robert Taunton (Wells Cathedral, 1662). As Stephen Bicknell pointed out, 'activity in 1660 simply restarted where it had stopped in 1642'[71] and fifteen or twenty years were to elapse before a new style was introduced. The Dallams (Robert, Ralph and George) and Thomas Harrison (soon to change his name to Harris) came back from France and tried to impose the French style. Charles II's support for French-inspired art enabled Thomas Harris and then his son Renatus from 1670 to obtain important contracts for the cathedrals of Gloucester (1663–65), Worcester (1666–67), Chichester (1667–68), and Hereford (1686).

'Father' Bernard Smith, who started working in London in 1667, is generally credited with introducing the new manner of organ building that was to dominate England until the early decades of the nineteenth century. He achieved

---

[69] See Bicknell, *History of the English Organ*, 30–4; Dominic Gwynn, 'The Origins of the English Style in Church Organ-Building', *B.I.O.S. Journal*, no. 30 (2006), 116–30; John Harper, 'An Organ for St Teilo: a Welsh Instrument in the Pre-Reformation Tradition', *B.I.O.S. Journal*, no. 35 (2011), 134–53.

[70] Nicholas Temperley, 'Organ Music in Parish Churches, 1660–1730', *B.I.O.S. Journal*, no. 5, 33.

[71] Stephen Bicknell, 'English Organ-Building 1642–1685', *B.I.O.S. Journal*, no. 5 (1981), 14.

a standard synthesis between elements borrowed from Germany and France, creating what was to become a distinctive national style. His rivalry with Renatus Harris is well documented. It reached its peak with the famous 'battle of the organs' between 1684 and 1688, during which the two organ builders each built an organ in the Temple Church, London, for the Benchers of the Temple to decide which one they would finally choose. The organs were demonstrated by reputed musicians, including John Blow and Henry Purcell, and bitter wrangling between the two clans lasted for several years. Eventually, the contract was awarded to Father Smith.[72] The difference in style between Smith and Harris reflected their respective backgrounds. Smith, who was born Baerent Smitt, came from Bremen. He had been organist at Hoorn in Holland, built the organ of the Grote Kerk at Edam, and arrived in England in 1667.[73] Renatus Harris, on the other hand, had family ties with the Dallams, who had escaped to France during the Commonwealth and whose style was therefore influenced by the aesthetic of the French organ tradition. Harris himself had spent his childhood in France[74] and arrived in England at the age of eight. The two major organ builders at the time of the Glorious Revolution (1688) were therefore immersed in foreign traditions. It is somewhat paradoxical that the English school of organ building, which appears so insular, should have been influenced by continental practices. These mixed roots account for the special character of the eighteenth-century English organ, at the crossroads between the North German and Dutch schools on the one hand, and the French on the other. Reeds and mixtures were introduced into the otherwise conservative specifications of new organs, since pre-Commonwealth techniques and styles survived, and the Restoration organ still echoed the traditional school.[75] Be that as it may, the newly established tradition was to remain almost unaltered until the end of the Georgian period. There was, naturally, a gradual evolution within that stylistic model: late eighteenth-century organs were undoubtedly more 'refined' than late-seventeenth- or early eighteenth-century instruments. The age of Hogarth is not that of Constable, nor the music of Handel the same as that of

---

[72] See Henry Leffler, *The Leffler Manuscript* (1800), facsimile edition with Introduction by Peter Williams (Reigate: British Institute of Organ Studies, 2010), 114–16; Bicknell, *History of the English Organ*, 128–30; David S. Knight, 'The Battle of the Organs, the Smith Organ at the Temple and its Organist', *B.I.O.S. Journal*, no. 21 (1997), 76–99.

[73] John Rowntree, 'Bernard Smith (c. 1629–1708) Organist and Organbuilder: His Origins', *B.I.O.S. Journal*, no. 2, 10–23.
See Bicknell, *History of the English Organ*, 128–30.

[74] Cecil Clutton and Austin Niland, *The British Organ* (London: Eyre Methuen, 1963/1982), 64.

[75] 'Both [Smith and Harris] found their style curtailed by contemporary taste, and that taste had been cultured by the previous generation of organ-builders. Thus, the work of Smith and Harris is only a small step away from that of their predecessors ... '. Bicknell, 'English Organ-Building 1642–1685', 6.

Thomas Linley, and it is therefore natural that organ building should have evolved, within the same stylistic paradigm, in the course of the century. A fine study of the technical evolution of English organs in the course of the long eighteenth century – which is outside the scope of the present study – would no doubt reveal subtle differences between the various organ builders' distinctive styles. However, the general format of the instrument remained consistent. The overall unity and stylistic coherence of the English organ in the eighteenth century, and the fact that its general characteristics remained more or less unchanged, suggests that the style of the instrument was far more than the result of haphazard historical circumstances. It perfectly fitted the needs, taste and conceptions of the contemporaneous society.

The period that followed the Glorious Revolution was one in which Britain felt and expressed a renewed sense of confidence and pride, with strong economic expansion and the development of wealthy, influential middle classes. It witnessed the rise of a 'polite and commercial people', to use Paul Langford's phrase,[76] in a society that tried to assert its cultural values and project a certain image of its power and wealth through artefacts and cultural practices. Public concerts developed in the metropolis and the main provincial cities and towns. In wealthy churches it was fashionable to erect an organ to accompany the singing of the congregation (and, in some places, a large choir of charity children). The presence of an organ was a reaction against the Puritan banishment of the instrument from churches during the Commonwealth. While music was now accepted again, its use being validated by numerous writings and sermons,[77] it was important that it should remain within the confines of decency, decorum and moderation, so as to preclude any accusation of fanaticism, excess or 'effeminacy', the most frequently used terms of disparagement against 'popery'. The tonal characteristic of the eighteenth-century English organ had to reflect the aspirations of contemporary society by expressing in aesthetic terms an ideologically informed 'middle way'.

There was undoubtedly a link between the intended role of the organ as an instrument dedicated to congregational accompaniment and its sonorous characteristics and qualities. It had to be 'full', that is, powerful enough to provide good support to the voices, yet not too loud or harsh. The profile of an instrument that had to be both full-bodied but relatively soft, and present without being overbearing, is outlined in the recommendations concerning its accompanying role. John Marsh gave the following advice for registration:

---

[76] Paul Langford, *A Polite and Commercial People – England 1727–1783* (Oxford: Oxford University Press, 1992).

[77] See Dubois, 'The Organ and Its Music Vindicated', *passim*.

The Diapasons may ... be considered as the Two Unisons and foundation of the whole Mixture, and must always be drawn, no other Stops being to be used without being joined with them, though they may themselves be used alone .... These five stops (the Diapasons, the Principal, the Twelfth and the Fifteenth) form a proper Mixture, to accompany the Choral Parts of the Services in Cathedrals in common, and to accompany a small Congregation in the Psalms in Parish Churches.[78]

Not only was the instrument designed within the bounds of moderation in terms of both the stop list and the voicing of the pipes, but the way of using it was also the object of prudent prescription. Numerous writers insisted on the necessity for the organist not to play too loud so as not to 'overpower' or 'drown' the voices. The Reverend Arthur Bedford, who wrote repeatedly against the stage and advocated a simple style of religious music, explained:

It would be very convenient in Parochial churches, that the organist did not play so loud whilst the Congregation is singing. The full Organ is generally too loud for a congregation, and drowns the voices that they are not heard. .... Art was only intended to help Nature, and not to overbear it. And instruments were design'd to direct our voices, not to drown them.[79]

For Burney, the right way of accompanying singers consisted in 'very judiciously suffering the voices to be heard in all their purity', to the point that one forgot that they were accompanied. This, he added, was 'the true style for the church', for 'it calls to memory nothing vulgar, light or prophane; it disposes the mind to philanthropy, and divests it of its gross and sensual passions' (*Music in France*, 152–3).

What such a comment reveals is that there was a close connection between aesthetic judgement and the assertion of particular moral values. Defined by its role as a liturgical instrument primarily meant to accompany the congregation and choir, the organ was supposed to avoid all risk of coarseness or lewdness, which had been the condition for it to be allowed back into the Church since the Restoration. Once mentalities had become accustomed again to the use of the organ in the Church, thanks both to the renewal of that practice and to various rhetorical and theoretical justifications, the organist was to play an increasingly pre-eminent part, while the organ 'remained the centre, as it were, of the musical world' in the eighteenth century.[80] In a letter to the *Gentleman's Magazine*, William Hayes, a 'member of Worcester Cathedral', talked of the 'despotic'

---

[78] John Marsh, 'Preface', *Eighteen Voluntaries for the Organ* (London, 1791), i.

[79] Arthur Bedford, *The Great Abuse of Musick* (London, 1711), 242.

[80] Jonathan Barry. 'Cultural Patronage and the Anglican Crisis: Bristol, c. 1689-1775', in John Walsh, Colin Haydon and Stephen Taylor, *The Church of England, c.1689-c.1833: From Toleration to Tractarianism* (Cambridge: Cambridge University Press, 1993), 194.

power of the organist over the congregation. He did not mean that the organist was to dominate by playing loudly but that he was the one from whom the singers would take their cue and the necessary impulsion.[81]

This quest for balance, moderation and refinement was grounded in religious and social motives, but it also corresponded to a philosophical and aesthetic agenda supported by numerous theoretical contributions in the course of the century.[82] Soon after the Restoration, John Locke's influential *Essay Concerning Human Understanding* (1690) had laid the theoretical foundation by showing that the logical corollary to a denunciation of the excesses of the 'Enthusiasts', who had caused so much harm to the country during the Interregnum, was to assert the benefits of moderation. He explained that, since human knowledge was so limited, all sectarian or fanatical opinion had to be proscribed. This grounded the ethos of moderation upon reason, which was to have lasting consequences in matters political, religious and aesthetic throughout the eighteenth century. Although its members were a minority, the Latitudinarian branch of Anglicanism, which was greatly influenced by Locke's outlook, prevailed during that period. John Tillotson, Archbishop of Canterbury, advocated a middle course in matters religious, and explained that he 'had much rather persuade any one to be a good man, than to be of any party or denomination of Christians whatsoever'.[83] For him, God, reason and nature proceeded from the same principles and he argued that 'everything is at rest and peace when it is that State which Nature intended it to be'.[84] Likewise, thinkers, poets, artists and writers asserted that taste had to be guided by 'Unerring Nature', as Alexander Pope put it in his *Essay on Criticism* of 1711.[85] They saw a logical chain between the notions of nature, truth and beauty. The rules of art were to be borrowed from nature herself ('Nature methodiz'd', Pope wrote). The lack of right proportions was seen as one of the most frequent causes of bad taste, and it followed logically that balance was seen as a requirement in matters of both taste and manners. The very fact of establishing taste upon ethical demands opened up the way towards an aesthetic of moderation, summed up for instance by the Scottish minister and philosopher Alexander Gerard:

> Correctness of taste preserves us from approving or disapproving any objects but such as possess the qualities which render them really laudable or blameable. ... Every excellence is a middle between two extremes, one of

---

[81] William Hayes, Letter to *The Gentleman's Magazine*, vol. 35 (1765), 213–14.

[82] See Dubois, *L'orgue dans la société anglaise, passim*.

[83] John Tillotson, Sermon XI, in *The Works* (London: James, John and Paul Knapton, 1735), vol. I.

[84] Tillotson, Sermon XII, in *The Works*, vol. I, p. 105.

[85] Alexander Pope, *An Essay on Criticism* (London: W. Lewis, 1711).

which always bears some likeness to it, and is apt to be confounded with it. The right and the wrong are not separated by an uncontested boundary. Like day and night, they run insensibly into one another: and it is often hard to fix the precise point where one ends, and the other begins.[86]

The theory of nature that ran in England through the eighteenth century resulted in the definition of a compelling aesthetic norm: if beauty borrowed its rules from the natural order and there was an ethical equation between the good and the beautiful, the artist had to conform to the aesthetic precepts he derived from his observation of nature. This is what the poet and philosopher James Beattie asserted: 'Poetry, therefore, and indeed every art whose end is to please, must be natural; and if so, must exhibit real matter of fact, or something like it; that is, in other words, must be, either according to truth, or according to verisimilitude'.[87] As a consequence moderation and simplicity were advocated as the condition for beauty and taste: 'Simplicity makes music, as well as language, intelligible and expressive. It is in every work of art a recommendatory quality. In music it is indispensable; for we are never pleased with that music which we cannot understand, or which seems to have no meaning.'[88] From the ethical point of view, moderation was advocated in eighteenth-century England as the best bulwark against both Puritan fanaticism and the excess perceived to be the defining characteristics of Catholic France and Italy. From John Locke onwards, most British thinkers and philosophers of the period advocated moderation as a necessity so as not to 'step outside the bonds of nature' or 'swell beyond proper bounds'.[89] 'The too much is incomprehensible as the too little, and a certain degree of greatness strikes us much in the same manner as vacuity', wrote John Donaldson in 1786.[90]

While this rhetoric of moderation, simplicity, balance and decency was expressed in philosophical treatises and essays on aesthetics as well as in sermons and religious exhortations, it also made its way into novels propounding these virtues as characteristically English. This is the case, for instance, of *Sir Charles Grandison* (1753), by Samuel Richardson, which portrays a 'perfectly good man'.[91] Richardson argued that sensibility leads to virtue. Sir Charles, the hero of the novel, is the paragon of reserve, moderation and self-

---

[86] Alexander Gerard, *An Essay on Taste* (Edinburgh, 1759, 3rd ed., London: Bell, Creech and Cadell, 1780), 125–6.

[87] James Beattie, *Essays on Poetry and Music as They Affect the Mind* (London: London: E. and C. Dilly and W. Creech, Edinburgh, 1779), 33.

[88] Beattie, *Essays on Poetry and Music*, 102.

[89] Henry Home, *Elements of Criticism* (London: T. Cadell and G. Robinson, 1761; 6th ed. Edinburgh: J. Bell and W. Creech), 241.

[90] John Donaldson, *Principles of Taste, or the Elements of Beauty* (Edinburgh, n.p.: 1786), 29.

[91] Samuel Richardson, *The History of Sir Charles Grandison* (London, 1753), ed. Jocelyn Harris (London: Oxford University Press, 1972).

control. Manhood was thus redefined according to a purely British set of values: being brave did not consist in overusing one's strength. And Handel's oratorio of *Alexander's Feast*, which explicitly served as a model for the novel, equally reasserted that ethos of moderation: Alexander's destructive passion is denounced while St Cecilia's serene composure, introduced by the organ that is supposed to moderate the passions of former styles, enables the music to reach its virtuous goal. As for the musical style of the piece, it avoids bombast or gratuitous virtuosity.[92]

Georgian organ music perfectly accorded with this definition of moderation. It was the transcription in aesthetic terms of the ethical imperative of moderation.[93] However, church music, and in particular organ music, was also constantly assumed, and required to be 'sublime' – under penalty of being dismissed as profane, lewd or frivolous. In his influential *Philosophical Enquiry into the Origin of our Ideas of the Sublime and Beautiful* (1757), Edmund Burke explained that the greatest source of aesthetic enjoyment was provided by the sublime. He opposed the beautiful and the sublime. For him, the sublime was a superior power that triggered a feeling of terror in man. To be able thus to create such strong reactions, the sublime object had to be extreme or excessive. The sublime could not be reconciled with what was 'mediocre'. Where sounds were concerned, Burke listed cataracts, storms, thunder or the sound of artillery as the main source of sublimity – that is natural, not musical sounds. Too shrill or loud a sound could not be pleasing, however. This led to the definition of the 'true sublime', as opposed to bombast or excess:

> the beautiful in music will not bear that loudness and strength of sounds, which may be used to raise other passions; nor notes, which are shrill, or harsh, or deep; it agrees best with such as are clear, even, smooth, and weak. .... great variety, and quick transitions from one measure or tone to another, are contrary to the genius of the beautiful in music. Such transitions often excite mirth, or other sudden and tumultuous passions; but not that sinking, that melting, that languor, which is the characteristical effect of the beautiful, as it regards every sense.[94]

Music, as opposed to natural sounds, belonged to the category of the beautiful, which was thought pleasant, soft and 'feminine', and, indeed, many aspects of the voluntaries composed at the time seem rather to belong to the category of

---

[92] For a more detailed discussion of this question, see Pierre Dubois, *Music in the Georgian Novel* (Cambridge: Cambridge University Press, 2015), 28–45.

[93] For a more detailed discussion of this question, see Dubois, *Music in the Georgian Novel*, 147–60.

[94] Edmund Burke, *A Philosophical Enquiry into the Origin of our Ideas of the Sublime and Beautiful*, 1757, ed. Adam Philips (Oxford & New York: Oxford University Press, 1990), 234.

the 'beautiful'. There was therefore a tension between the (pre-Romantic) cult of the sublime (which led to the Gothic) and the criteria of moderation we have thus far analysed. The English organ of the period thus tried dialectically to reconcile the two poles of sublimity and the beautiful within a paradigm of moderation. The deep, grave sounds of the organ could inspire a sense of awe and solemnity and the Church tried to insist on the necessity for religious music to be sublime so that it could 'lift' the soul. The swelling of a sound was thought to be a cause of the sublime. The passage from soft to loud or loud to soft was considered the best means of attaining the sublime, which partly explains the rise in England of the swell pedal in organs (see below in Section 6):

> so notes gradually swelling, and gradually decaying, have an agreeable effect on the ear and on the mind; the former tending to rouse the faculties, and the latter to compose them; the one promoting gentle exercise, and the other rest.[95]

Conversely, since excess was aesthetically and ethically proscribed, the organ had to remain within the due bounds of moderation. The demand for sublimity was therefore partly checked by other strong aesthetic criteria that were thought to be equally important in purely musical terms.

Such is the philosophical context within which Burney's comments on organs and organists can best be apprehended, and also the theoretical backdrop to his preferences in musical styles, as we shall now discover.

4 Questions of Style

In his *History of Music*, Burney repeatedly lambasted composers whose style he found too complex, stilted and lacking in graceful melody. Of Thomas Tallis he wrote that his two compositions preserved in Queen Elizabeth's Virginal Book are 'alike dry, elaborate and difficult, to hands formed by modern Music. The little melody and rhythm in the compositions of these times required all the harmony that could be crowded into them. Notes are multiplied without end, and difficulties created without effect' [*History*, II, 66]. He passed the same judgement on William Byrd and John Bull: of the former, Burney wrote that 'at the period in which he flourished, nothing seems to have been thought necessary for keyed-instruments, except variations to old tunes, in which all the harmony was crowded, which the singers could grasp, and all the rapid divisions of the times which they could execute. Even nominal *Fancies* were without fancy, and confined to the repetition of a few dry and unmeaning notes in fugue, or imitation' [*History*, II, 78]. As for Bull, though Burney would greatly admire

---

[95] Beattie, *Essays on Poetry and Music*, 150.

'the hand, as well as patience, of any one capable of playing his compositions', his music 'would afford [him] no kind of pleasure. *Ce sont des notes & rien que des notes*; there is nothing in them which excites rapture. They may be heard by a lover of Music with as little emotion as the clapper of a mill, or the rumbling of a postchaise' (*History*, II, 96). Burney was decidedly and unashamedly a 'modern', who thought the music of the past was unbearably dry, artificial and austere. For, he explained, 'Melody, itself the child of Fancy, was still held in Gothic chains.' He argued that 'as the confining Music merely to religious purposes borders on fanaticism; so the treating secular and light subjects with ecclesiastical gravity; making a fugue of every movement, and regarding grace, elegance, and fertility of invention, as criminal, or, at best, as frivolous, are equally proofs of want of taste, and want of candour' (*History*, II, 128). The underlying question was what he considered to be *natural*. Like Rousseau, Burney esteemed that melody was the primary source of music, and that harmony was only subservient to it. For him, too-elaborate harmony was therefore detrimental to the natural effect of melody: 'The pedantry of crude harmonies and learned modulation, only suits depraved ears that are grown callous to every thing that is easy and natural' (*History*, II, 258).

Thus, Burney thought that simplicity was 'necessary to the longevity in musical compositions', as he wrote in a letter to his friend Thomas Twining. Purcell's music soon grew 'obsolete' because he wrote down 'all the fashion-able graces and embellishments of his time', and 'it is not so easy, nor perhaps warrantable, to simplify Music, as to embroider & adorn it' (*Letters*, 'To Thomas Twining', 21 January 1774). Interestingly, Burney justified his con-demnation of 'complicated contrivances' and his plea in favour of simplicity by appealing to the judgement of the greater number, suggesting that intricate musical compositions could not appeal to the multitude and were only intended for the educated few who were able to understand their elaborate technicalities. What must predominate, therefore, was 'grace and tranquil harmony, instead of disguise and suffocation', as the Italians showed by simplifying their secular music. He thought that the music of the past was irretrievably lost to modern hearers, who would find it unintelligible, and that there was 'as little chance for a musician of the present age to perform such productions in the manner of the times in which they were composed, as to pronounce a foreign language as well as his own; and if, against all calculation, he should succeed, this Music will still be an unknown tongue to the public' (*History*, II, 258–9). No doubt Burney would have been sceptical about our contemporary endeavours to recapture the essence and spirit of 'early music'!

The epitome of this ancient, learned style of music loathed by Burney seems to have been the fugue: 'Good canons and fugues can be produced but by few, yet as many have disgraced the invention by ignorance and dullness, the study of them is now almost wholly laid aside as Gothic invention' (*History*, II, 415). He thought that, because church music must be grave, the serious solemnity of the organ fugue was acceptable; however, as his own compositional attempts in the genre confirm (*History*, II, 285): 'though good taste has banished fugue, canon, and elaborate compositions from Dramatic Music, yet sound judgment has still retained them in the Church; to which, from the little use that is made of them elsewhere, they are now in a manner appropriated' (*History*, II, 161). Still, Burney generally condemned the complexity of the German style of organ music. Not even J. S. Bach, considered today as the greatest composer of all time for the organ, escaped his criticism. Quoting Quantz and Marpurg, Burney did concede that 'all the musical writers of Germany, for these last fifty years, have given testimony to his [J. S. Bach's] abilities' (*Music in Germany*, II, 81). He went on to relate the famous episode of the challenge between Marchand and Bach, concluding that 'it was an honour for Pompey that he was conquered by Caesar, and to Marchand to be only vanquished by Bach' (*Music in Germany*, II, 82). Yet, while Burney obviously admired Bach, he never sincerely warmed to his style of composition. Only in later years, and partly through the influence of his friend Samuel Wesley, was Burney to show more admiration for Bach than he had initially done and to make amends for his original statements.[96] Until then, he did not like the complexity of Bach's compositions and his constant use of canon and fugue, which Burney thought were not natural musical forms. Bach, 'though unequalled in learning and contrivance, thought it so necessary to crowd into both hands all the harmony he could grasp, that he must inevitably have sacrificed melody and expression' (*Music in Germany*, II, 263). While Burney readily admitted that 'among organists of the present century, Handel and Sebastian Bach are the most renowned', he wrote that Bach seems 'to have been constantly in search of what was new and difficult, without the least attention to nature and facility. He was fond of full harmony, that besides a constant and active use of the pedals, he is said to have put down such keys by a stick in his mouth, as neither hands nor feet could reach' (*History*, II, 953). Burney objected to full and intricate harmonies and preferred what was 'easy and graceful':

> The very terms of *Canon* and *Fugue* imply restraint and labour. Handel was perhaps the only great Fughist, exempt from pedantry. He seldom treated barren or crude subjects; his themes being almost always natural and pleasing. Sebastian Bach, on the contrary, like Michael Angelo in painting,

[96] See F. G. E., 'Dr Charles Burney (1726–1814). A Biographical Sketch (Concluded)', *The Musical Times*, vol. 45, no. 739 (1 Sep., 1904), 575–80. https://doi.org/10.2307/902828.

disdained facility so much, that his genius never stooped to the easy and graceful. I never have seen a fugue by this learned and powerful author upon a *motive*, that is not loaded with crude and difficult accompaniments. (*History* II, 96)

After noting that Bach produced 'many excellent compositions for the church', Burney mentioned the composer's '*Ricercare*, consisting of preludes, and fugues, for the organ, upon two, three, and four subjects; in *Modo recto & contrario*, and in every one of twenty-four keys', before remarking that 'all the present organ-players of Germany are formed upon his school, as most of those on the harpsichord, clavichord, and *piano-forte* are upon that of his son, the admirable Carl. Phil. Emanuel Bach' (*Music in Germany*, II, 81–3).[97] Burney observed that 'the passion for learned and polyphonic Music was not so early discountenanced by a partiality for simple melody in the cultivation of the musical drama in this country as in Italy, the reign of harmony and fugue continued much longer uninterrupted' (*History*, II, 456). Consequently, Burney insisted repeatedly upon the superiority of Handel, who will 'ever stand superior to all other writers' (*Music in France*, 164–5). In the *Account of . . . the Commemoration of Handel*, he asserted that 'in his full, masterly, and excellent *organ-fugues*, upon the most natural and pleasing subjects, [Handel] has surpassed Frescobaldi, and even Sebastian Bach, and others of his country-men, the most renowned for abilities in this difficult and elaborate species of compositions' (*Account*, 41). Intricacy, difficulty or complexity were anathema to Burney because they lacked in that moderation and natural simplicity considered so essential in his time.

5 Burney's Musical Travels 1: Foreign Organists

Before writing his *General History of Music*, Charles Burney decided to undertake a long tour of Europe in order to collect historical material and musical scores from the countries in which Western music had developed over the course of time. As he explained to his friend the actor David Garrick, his purpose was 'to get, from the libraries to the viva voce conversation of the learned, what information [he] could relative to the music of the ancients; and [. . .] to judge with [his] own eyes of the present state of modern music in the

---

[97] The same observation is taken up in the *History of Music*: 'In organ-playing and composition, Handel and Sebastian Bach seem not only to have surpassed their contemporaries, but to have established a style for that instrument which is still respected and imitated by the greatest organists in Germany. The harpsichord Music of these great masters gave way, about the middle of the century, to the more elegant and expressive compositions of C. P. Emanuel Bach, who was soon imitated so universally in Germany by writers for keyed-instruments, that there have been few works published since them since, which are not strongly tinctured with his style . . . ' (*History*, II, 951).

places through which [he] should pass, from the performance and conversation of the first musicians … ' [*Letters*, 'To David Garrick', Naples, 17 October 1770 – 18 October 1770]. Equipped with letters of recommendation to ambassadors and ministers occupying posts abroad, he first travelled around France and Italy in 1770, and then around Germany and the Netherlands in 1772, before beginning work on his *General History of Music* in 1773. Before doing so, however, he decided upon his return from the continent to publish a small volume on the 'Present State of Music in France and Italy', based upon his travel notebooks, as he announced to David Garrick in the same letter dated 17 October 1770:

> As my general History must be a work of Time, I intend publishing, as soon as I get Home, in a Pamphlet or small volume, an Account of the Present State of Music in France & Italy, in wch I shall describe according to my Judgment & Feelings the merits of the several Compositions & performers I have heard in travelling thro' those Countries. (*Letters*, 'To David Garrick', Naples, 17 October 1770 – 18 October 1770)

In another letter dated 28 February 1771, addressed to Pierre Guy to thank him for having arranged a meeting with Rousseau, Burney also mentioned his project of writing an account of his travel in France, of which he intended to make Rousseau the hero (*Letters*, 'To Pierre Guy', 1 Queen Square, 28 February 1771). As Edward Green has remarked, 'read as an autobiographical novel rather than as a repository of musicological information, [Burney's *History of Music*] takes on the quality of a quest. When Burney eventually finds Rousseau at last and the quest is therefore successful, 'the "novel" draws quickly to a close.'[98]

The Present State of Music in France and Italy was published in London in 1771 (followed by a second edition in 1773) and *The Present State of Music in Germany, the Netherlands, and United Provinces* in 1773 (followed by a second edition in 1775).[99] These travel books, which were very well received upon publication, constitute a unique account of the musical practices in Europe during the second half of the eighteenth century and are therefore of considerable interest for musical historians. In addition, the notebooks themselves, which differ somewhat from the published books, bring complementary information and deserve to be consulted. Burney's description of the organs he saw abroad and his accounts of his meetings with various foreign organists he was able to approach enable us to formulate a precise image of his own conception

---

[98] Edward Green, 'The Impact of Rousseau on the *Histories* of Burney and Hawkins: A Study in the Ethics of Musicology', in *Music's Intellectual History* (New York: RILM, 2009), 3.

[99] Recent editions have been published by Cambridge University Press.

of the instrument and the qualities he expected to find in both organs and organists. As he wrote, his 'intention was neither to write a panegyric, nor a satire, on the music of Germany, but to describe its effects on [his] feelings', and this would naturally apply to the music of the other countries he visited (*Music in Germany*, II, 339–40).

In the course of his journeys around Europe, Burney met numerous organists. His account of their respective abilities and styles builds up into a coherent plea in favour of simplicity and grace as opposed to formal complexity, which ties in well with his preferences in matters of musical styles. Though he would admit that some performers he heard in Germany were technically competent, the general tenor of his observations reveals a marked predilection for musicians endowed with a gift for invention and fancy, rather than those indulging in elaborate and abstruse counterpoint. Thus it is in terms of this opposition between what is natural and what is 'laboured' or 'affected' that Burney criticised Müller, the court organist at Dessau, who was 'possessed of considerable abilities, [and whose] compositions discover taste, fancy, and a powerful hand', but whose 'ambition to produce *new* passages, upon all occasions, render[ed] his pieces frequently laboured, unnatural, and affected. To this vice may be added that, so common to his countrymen, of spinning his subjects and movements to tiresome length' (*Music in Germany*, II, 327).

Burney often used the adjective 'masterly' to describe the performance of organists who impressed him, as for instance when writing about Christlieb Siegmund Binder in Dresden (see Section 6), or Johann Dulsick, organist at Czaslau in Bohemia, whom he heard play 'an admirable voluntary on the organ' with 'an extempore *fugue*, upon a new, and pleasing subject, in a very masterly manner'. He found the organist one of the best 'performers on the organ, which [*sic*] [he, Burney] heard throughout his journey' (*Music in Germany*, II, 5). Though Burney was often critical of organists playing in the manner of the Bach organ school, because he found that too many parts crowded the discourse and rendered it uselessly confused, he praised Mr Bertuch, the organist of St Peter's, Berlin, because he had 'a strong hand, and great knowledge of the instrument'. After playing extempore, Mr Bertuch 'executed a most learned and difficult double fugue, composed by old Bach [i.e. J. S.], expressly for the use of organs with pedals' (*Music in Germany*, I, 205–6).

One of the longest passages in his *Present State of Music in Germany and the Netherlands* is devoted to Pothoff, the blind organist of the Oude Kerk (Old Church) in Amsterdam, whose real name was Jacob Potholt (1720–82) (*Music in Germany*, II, 287–94). Potholt, who had previously been organist of the Westerkerk in Amsterdam from 1743 and was also carillonneur of the City Hall, was appointed at the Oude Kerk in 1766. Not well known today, he only set organ accompaniments for psalms and presented a few manuscript symphonies to the collegium musicum of Utrecht.[100] Burney was impressed by the talent of this 'admirable organist' whose 'hand, taste, and abilities in every particular are truly astonishing'. The Oude Kerk organ, a sixteen-foot instrument completed by Batti of Utrecht twelve years before Burney's visit, contained sixty-four stops on three manuals and pedals and its touch was 'the heaviest that [Burney] ever felt, each key requiring almost two-pound weight to put it down'. Nonetheless, 'such is the force of M. Pothoff's hand, that he plays this organ with as much lightness and rapidity, as if it were a common harpsichord'. What Burney undoubtedly admired in Pothoff's manner was that 'his taste [was] of the best modern kind'. Burney fully adhered to the modern, *galant* style of his age, hence his dislike for the grave contrapuntal complexity of the J. S. Bach organ school. Originally an admirer of Handel, Burney was open to the modern music of his time, and in particular Italian music, and he was later to champion the music of Haydn. He liked the fact that Pothoff's 'fancy [was] extremely lively' and that 'although he play[ed] very full, seldom in less than five parts, with the manuals and pedals together, yet, it [was] neither in the dry nor crude way, which [he, Burney] had so frequently heard in Germany'. Burney explained that Pothoff was a disciple of Locatelli, a composer/ virtuoso who had 'delighted in capricious difficulties', but that the organist also 'had a fund of knowledge, in the principles of harmony, that rendered such wild flights agreeable'. Pothoff played two fugues in a 'masterly manner, the subjects of which he reversed and turned to a thousand ingenious purposes'. What Burney really admired was the organist's energy and 'divine enthusiasm, which alone can transport an artist beyond the bounds of mediocrity'. Although he found the organist of the Oude Kerk, Mr Stechwech, a 'neat performer', he remarked that he was 'not possessed of that fire and invention, which characteris[ed] the Voluntaries of Mr. Pothoff'. Burney mentioned that Potholt was appointed at the Westerkerk after a competition in which he beat the other twenty-two candidates, and, in a note, compared this success to the appointment of John Stanley at St Andrew's, Holborn, in 1726. For Burney, incidentally, the organ was an instrument particularly adapted 'in its construction for the display of great musical talents, after the privation of sight', which he illustrated by giving the examples of Salinas, Milton, Handel, Potholt and Stanley (*History*, II, 239).

In Paris during his first tour, after going to Notre-Dame and the Concert Spirituel, Burney chose to go and listen to 'the celebrated Claude Balbastre' perform on his organ at St-Roch (spelt Saint-Roque by Burney) (*Music in France*, 36). Claude Balbastre (often mistakenly called Claude-Bénigne) was

---

[100] Rudolf A. Rasch, *The New Grove Dictionary of Music and Musicians* (2nd edition), ed. Stanley Sadie (London: Macmillan Publishers, 2001), vol. 20, 219–20.

born in Dijon on 8 December 1724. In 1750, he left Dijon and settled in Paris, where he enjoyed the protection and benefitted from the teaching of his country-man Jean-Philippe Rameau, and he soon acquired an excellent reputation, being celebrated for the 'lightness' and 'delicacy' of his touch. He became the first organist of the Concert Spirituel in 1755, where until 1772 he performed transcriptions and the first-ever organ concertos played in France. He was appointed organist at St-Roch in 1756, and then at Notre-Dame in 1760, alongside Armand-Louis Couperin, Louis-Claude Daquin and Foucquet. In 1762, he was ordered by Archbishop Christophe de Beaumont du Repaire to abstain from performing *Noëls* on the organ at Christmas because it drew too large a crowd and caused disorder.

Such was the musician, at the height of his powers, whose performance on the organ Burney was so curious to hear in Paris. In his notebooks as well as in the published version of the *Present State of Music in France and Italy*, Burney narrated his meeting with the French virtuoso, and the two complementary accounts shed an interesting light on Balbastre's style and practice during a church service. No particular piece played by Balbastre is mentioned and one understands that, following a tradition long established in France, the organist would improvise throughout the service rather than perform written-out pieces. Balbastre accompanied the choir and improvised between each verse of the Magnificat, which was the common liturgical practice in France at the time (*Music in France*, 21). Burney found that the organist he had heard at Notre-Dame the previous Thursday played in an 'old-fashioned style'. By contrast, he noted the variety of the styles and genres used by Balbastre, who played 'several minuets, fugues, imitations, and every species of music, even to hunting pieces and jigs, without surprising, or offending the congregation, as far as [he, Burney] was able to discover' (*Music in France*, 38) and who therefore appeared more 'modern' than his colleague Armand-Louis Couperin. Both the style of organ playing, and the mentalities of audiences and performers concerning its music and its use, were changing. The growing secularisation of society had a bearing on the evolution of church music, which was reflected in what Burney heard of Balbastre's style of playing. Although Burney generally tended to be dismissive of the French style of music, especially vocal music (*Letters*, 'To Denis Diderot', 1771), Balbastre seems to have escaped the brunt of his criticism.

So did his friend and colleague at Notre-Dame, Armand-Louis Couperin (1727–89), who was also organist both at the Ste-Chapelle and at St-Gervais, as his uncle François had been:

> M. Couperin accompanied the *Te Deum*, which was only chanted, with great abilities. The interludes between each verse were admirable. Great variety of stops and style, with much learning and knowledge of the instrument, were

shewn, and a finger equal in strength and rapidity to every difficulty. Many things of effect were produced by the two hands, up in the treble, while the base was played on the pedals. (*Music in France*, 40)

Burney seems however to have been more impressed by the style of Italian organists than by either French or German and Dutch ones, which ties in well with his preference for the simplicity and fancy of Italian music generally. He writes that 'with regard to the organ, [he] frequently [heard] it judiciously and spiritedly played in Italy': 'At Milan, San Martini has a way peculiar to himself of touching that instrument, which is truly masterly and pleasing. The first organists of St Marc's church at Venice, of the Duomo at Florence, and of St John Lateran at Rome ... are very superior in their performance to most others I have heard on the continent' (*Music in France*, 298–300). He praised Signor G. Corbeli, the first organist at the Duomo in Florence, who played in 'a masterly grave style, suited to the place and instrument' (*Music in France*, 80). His only complaint concerned noisy accompaniments, which he denounced repeatedly: 'There is a general complaint in England against loud accompaniments: and, if an evil there, it is doubly such in Italy' (*Music in France*, 104). The organ should not overpower the voices of the choir or congregation, a criticism that was also extremely frequent in the sermons on church music at the time, as we have seen, and is also present in the recommendations of John Marsh, John Antes La Trobe and Joseph Warren, among others. In St Antonio in Padua, Burney found that 'two of the four organs were more than sufficient to over-power the voices; and ... it were to be wished that [the organists] would accompany the voices and instruments, which are good, and well worth hearing, with the choir organs only, as we do in England; for otherwise, nothing *but* the organs can be heard: they are indeed fine-toned instruments, but so powerful, as to render all the rest of the performance useless' (*Music in France*, 141–2). In another place, Burney remarked that 'there was more pretty music badly performed. The organ, by executing all the symphonies and accompaniments, overpowered the violins, and had a bad effect, though neatly played' (*Music in France*, 374).

6 Burney's Musical Travels 2: Foreign Organs

A striking aspect of the eighteenth-century English organ was its relatively small size, especially when compared to that of its continental counterparts. The two largest cathedral organs around 1800 were those of St Paul's and York Minster, each containing twenty-seven stops, and the largest organ in England at that time was that of Christ Church, Spitalfields, built by Richard Bridge in 1735, which originally boasted only thirty stops (after a long period of disuse, fortunately this organ was restored by William Drake's team in

2015).[101] Organs that were considered quite sizeable by the English standards of the eighteenth century, such as those of the Foundling Hospital
(Thomas Parker, 1769) and St Anne's Limehouse (Richard Bridge, 1741) –
the organist of both being William Russell at the turn of the nineteenth
century – had no more than twenty-eight and twenty-six stops respectively.
This was a far cry from the organs of Notre-Dame, Paris (François Thierry,
1733, forty-six stops), St-Martin, Tours (Lefebvre, 1761, sixty-three stops),
or St-Sulpice, Paris (François-Henri Clicquot, 1781, sixty-three stops) in
France; St Bavo, Haarlem (Müller, 1738, sixty stops) in the Netherlands; and
St Martin, Weingarten (Gabler, 1750, sixty-three stops) or St Jacobi,
Hamburg (Schnitger, 1760, sixty stops) in Germany, to cite just a few of
the most famous continental instruments of the period. In a letter to the
Gentleman's Magazine in 1772, the clergyman and mathematician William
Ludlam wrote:

> We are apt to be astonished at what is told of the immense size of the foreign
> organs, which have always four rows of keys, beside pedals; but when we are
> informed that these keys go no lower than cc, and that the ranks of the larger
> pipes are not completed to the bottom, the wonder ceases. In fact, these great
> organs are filled with nothing but a repetition of the smaller and less harmo-
> nious stops, and some others that are meer whims. Neither have any of these
> foreign organs a swell. See the description of that in the abbey of
> Weingarthen, by D. Bedos. This organ has in it 6666 pipes. The whole
> number of stops is 66, among which are the fiddle, the drum, the cuckow,
> the nightingale, and the roaring of the sea. *Risum teneatis*? (i.e. 'can you help
> laughing?')[102]

It is interesting to contrast the largest continental organs with the organ
erected jointly by Christopher Schrider and Abraham Jordan in Westminster
Abbey in 1730, which, apart from the addition of thirteen pedals at a later stage,
was to remain almost untouched until 1848. It is amazing to think that only
twenty-three stops were deemed sufficient to fill such a vast building (Table 5).

The English organ of the period was essentially centred around the Great
Chorus (Open and Stopped Diapasons, Principal, Twelfth, Fifteenth). The
manuals could not be coupled together, so it was impossible to add up the
different divisions for greater effect. For the 'Full Organ' registration, the
Sesquialtera and Mixture could be added and sometimes (but not systematic-
ally) the Trumpet. The English organ of the period was not weak, however, and

---

[101] Charles W. Pearce, *Notes on English Organs of the Period 1800–1810* (London: The Vincent
        Music Company Ltd, 1912), 3–4; Ian Bell, 'Elegant Sufficiency', *Choir and Organ*, vol. 23, no.
        5 (September/October 2015), 18–22.
[102] William Ludlam, Letter to *The Gentleman's Magazine*, December 1772, vol. 24, 562–5.

Table 5 Westminster Abbey: Stop list[*]

Great	Choir	Echos/Swell
Open Diapason	Principal, in front Gilt	Open Diapason
Open Diapason	Stop[d] Diapason	Quintadena
Stop[d] Diapason	Flute	Principal
Principal	Fifteenth	Flageolet
Twelfth	Cremona	Trumpet
Fifteenth		Vox Humana
Nason		
Sesquialtera IV		
Trumpet		
Clarion		
Mixture		
Cornet V		

[*] Source: David S. Knight, 'The Organs of Westminster Abbey and Their Music, 1240–1908', Ph. D., Historical Musicology (King's College, University of London, 2001), I, 61-2.

it was 'capable of providing a virile sound', as William Drake put it,[103] but builders aimed at a singing, unforced quality of sound. Though not very large, eighteenth-century English organs 'were, in their way, very sophisticated: mechanically orderly and accomplished, well made and very carefully voiced', as Stephen Bicknell wrote.[104]

It is quite striking that both William Ludlam, as late as 1772, and Burney, in his *History of Music* (*History*, II, 343–4), should still mention Father Smith as the model they chose to emulate, which testifies to their attachment to a well-established national tradition and school of organ building. Ludlam contrasted noise with harmony and also rejected the very principle of breaks in the Furnitures and Cymbals because he thought these breaks made a clear perception of the fundamental basis of harmony impossible and also, probably, because they did not correspond to a 'rational' disposition.[105] The principle of breaks can indeed be interpreted as the manifestation of the precedence of illusion in baroque epistemology since lower octaves are taken up as one goes

---

[103] Mark Linley and William Drake, 'Grosvenor Chapel and the 18th-Century Organ', *B.I.O.S. Journal*, no. 15 (1991), 90–117 (90).

[104] Bicknell, *History of the English Organ*, 213.

[105] Because mixtures tend to be quite high-pitched stops, the smaller, higher pipes at the top of the range are difficult to hear, as well as so small as to be almost impracticable for the builders to make. Consequently, it is common practice to 'break' back the highest ranks and repeat the previous octave of pipes at the lower pitch level.

up the scale without the ear perceiving these returns, as the fundamental keeps rising. It seems that there was a certain degree of reluctance in England towards a principle of registration that appeared, as it were, 'illogical', and that shocked both the ears and the mind. It is interesting to observe that this reluctance lasted for a long time since, even though organ-building practices had evolved considerably by then, Hopkins and Rimbault wrote around 1877: 'The large stops increase the fullness, roundness, depth and sonority of the organ, imparting great richness to the general effect; whereas more Mixture may increase the "din" of the organ to such an extent as to be almost intolerable.'[106]

Thus, characteristically, Burney expressed great surprise at the size of the massive instruments he saw on the continent, which tended to be much larger than those in England. For him, the multiplication of stops and ranks was not only useless but clearly detrimental to the beauty of the sound produced, and he denounced the bad tuning of the organs he heard in Berlin, which produced noise rather than harmony: 'In general, I found the organs of Berlin large, coarse, and crowded with noisy stops, which, if they had been in tune, would have produced no pleasing effects; but as it was, such a number of dissonant and ill-voiced pipes, more tortured than tickled the ear' (*Music in Germany*, III, 103). Burney found that the organ at St Peter's, Berlin, an instrument funded by the late king and 'intended to be the largest in the world', but never completed, was too powerful for the building 'even in this diminished state', and that, because of the reverberation, 'all [was] confused and indistinct' (*Music in Germany*, I, 205). In France, though he acknowledged that the organ of St-Gervais in Paris, erected by Clicquot, was 'a very good one', he felt that the reverberation in the large church rendered everything 'indistinct and confused' (*Music in France*, 26). Incidentally, Burney expressed the same detestation for excessive echo and a marked preference for clear, articulate sounds when he heard Mme Brillon play the fortepiano in Paris in 1770, complaining that he 'could not persuade Madame B. to play the piano forte with the stops on' (i.e. the dampers) for 'with them off unless in arpeggios, nothing is distinct – 'tis like the sound of bells, continual and confluent' (*Music, Men, and Manners*, 20).

Burney emphasised a correlation between the characteristics of the instruments and the style of execution they afforded organists. For him, the lack of fancy of German organists was closely linked to the excessive size and cumbersome touch of their large instruments. He thought the multiplication of ranks speaking together stiffened the touch. Although he found the organ at Haarlem (see later on in this section) 'a noble instrument', he commented that 'all these

---

[106] Edward J. Hopkins and F. Rimbault, *The Organ, its History and Construction; a Comprehensive Treatise on the Structure and Capabilities of the Organ* (London: Robert Cocks & Co., 1855, 3rd ed. 1877), 53.

enormous machines seem loaded with useless stops, or such as only contribute to augment noise, and to stiffen the touch' (*Music in Germany*, 310; *Cyclopedia*, vol. 25, n.p.). The organ in Dresden is a case in point as 'the multiplicity of stops in this organ, mounting to 54, only augments noise, and adds to the weight of the touch', while there are 'very few solo stops that are agreeable', and 'no *swell* has ever been heard of in an organ at Dresden' (*Music in Germany*, III, 54–6). Similarly, in Hamburg, the massive Hildebrand thirty-two-foot organ of St Michael's (sixty-four stops on four manuals and pedals), which he thought was 'the largest and most complete in Europe' (*Music in Germany*, II, 274), failed to please him completely. Although he found the chorus 'the most noble that can be imagined', he considered it 'more striking by its force, and the richness of the harmony, than by a clear and distinct melody, which fashion makes it necessary to load with a crowd of accompaniments in all German churches' (*Music in Germany*, II, 275).

Another recurring criticism from Burney about foreign organs (and harpsi-chords) was that their keyboard action was too noisy. He wrote that 'to persons accustomed to English harpsichords, all the keyed instruments on the continent appear to a great disadvantage'. In Italy, the keys of the spinets are 'so noisy, and the tone is so feeble, that more wood is heard than wire', he explained (*Music in France*, 298). In France, he also disliked the noise made by the action of the organ at St-Roch in Paris (*Music in France*, 37–8), and even found the keys of Balbastre's own chamber organ as noisy as those at St-Roch (*Music in France*, 40–2).

In the *Cyclopedia*, Burney explained that the bellows 'should at all times give an equal weight of wind … without which no organ can ever be in tune: also, when carefully blown, no difference should be heard from the action of blow-ing' (*Cyclopedia*, vol. 25, n.p.). While he often denounced the 'coarseness' of foreign instruments, he also deplored their being poorly played and out of tune:

> After dinner I went to the church of Santa Maria Maggiore to see some pictures, and stumbled on music, but such music as I did not think it possible for the people of Italy to bear. The organ was out of tune, other instruments out of time, and the voices were both; then the composition seemed just such stuff as a boy who was learning counter-point would produce after the first two or three lessons. (*Music in France*, 182)

In the richly ornamented Church of San Michele in Bologna, the organ was playing when he entered to a procession, 'but it was out of tune, and coarse, and not well played' (*Music, Men, and Manners*, 88). He 'did not meet with one single organ in the whole town [of Antwerp] that was in tune' (*Music in Germany*, I, 35). In the Dominican church, there were two organs, 'esteemed the best in the town'. He 'found the pipes of these instruments well toned, but so miserably out of tune, as to give more pain than pleasure to the hearer' (*Music in Germany*, I, 32–3). In Frankfurt, he noted that the organ was 'no[t] ill-toned, but, like most of the others which [he] had heard in [his] route, miserably out of tune, and the touch so heavy, that the keys, like those of a *carillon*, severally required the weight of the whole hand, to put them down' (*Music in Germany*, I, 77). He also found the organ in the church of St-Gaetano in Venice 'coarse, and poorly played' and went on to criticise the voices which 'consisted only of two indifferent tenors and a base', while the 'composition was very common, and unmarked by any stamp of original genius' (*Music in France*, 157).

It is clear that, curious and open-minded though he was, Burney was not very objective. In spite of (apparently) genuine interest for foreign usages and practices, those were the object of global misunderstanding and almost systematic criticism. This is obvious as concerns the use of pedals, which Burney found 'a very laborious business'. English organs did not have pedals. When he travelled across various European countries, Burney saw and heard continental organists play on the pedals, which was a novelty for him. The lack of elegance in the organist's demeanour, the effort required, the technical difficulty which he thought proved detrimental to the grace and fancy that ought to characterise the touch of a good organist, all of these contributed to Burney's feeling that pedals were a useless adjunct. His description of this practice testifies to the rejection and even a kind of disgust inspired in him:

> [The organist, Mr. Binder] played three or four fugues in a very full and masterly manner, making great use of the pedals. I did not indeed find him possessed of much fancy; but in the German manner of playing, there is not much opportunity of shewing it. To use the pedals of these huge instruments much, at the same time as two hands are fully employed on the stiff and heavy manuals, is a very laborious business. The multiplicity of stops in this organ, amounting to 54, only augments noise, and adds to the weight of the touch . . . [Mr. Binder], when he had done, was in as violent a heat with fatigue and exertion, as if he had run eight or ten miles, full-speed, over ploughed lands in the dog-days. (*Music in Germany*, 147–8)

Burney was more interested in soft solo stops and the expressive swell mechanism than in the sheer power of the chorus. Thus, he expressed strong reservations about the organ in Ulm Minster, built by Johann Matthaus Schmahl and containing 45 stops, on three sets of keys and pedals, with 3,442 pipes. The size of the instrument was not enough to win him over. Although the organ was 'so much celebrated by travellers, for size and goodness, that it excited in [him] a great desire to see and examine it, [he] was somewhat disappointed in finding it neither so ancient, so large, nor so full of stops, as [he] expected'. He noted that 'the German flute seems the best of the solo stops', and the 'reed-work is pretty good' but deplored the fact that there was no swell (*Music in Germany*, I, 114). For indeed England enjoyed a device unknown to the rest of Europe – the swell mechanism. Introduced by the Jordans (father and son) on the organ of St Magnus the Martyr, London Bridge, in 1712, the swell mechanism became a key feature of the Georgian organ. Characteristically for an eighteenth-century author, Burney believed in progress in art, and he saw the swell as a distinct sign of the advancement of Britain in both organ building, and musical taste. The absence of a similar device on continental instruments relegated them to the rank of relics of the past:

> It is very extraordinary that the swell, which has been introduced into the English organ more than fifty years, and which is so capable of expression and of pleasing effects, that it may well be called the greatest and most important improvement that ever was made on any keyed instrument, should be still utterly unknown in Italy. (*Music in France*, 387)

The organ of St Michael's, Hamburg, did have a swell, but Burney mentioned that it produced very little effect (*Music in Germany*, II, iv, 275–6). Contrary to Francis Routh, who wrote that the swell was a 'purely mechanical invention, whose origin was in the mind of an organ builder, and was of little or no concern to composers of organ music',[107] I would argue that this device reflected a deeply felt concern for expression as a central issue – at both practical and theoretical levels – among eighteenth-century English musicians. The idea was to render the organ more expressive thanks to crescendo and decrescendo effects of the kind that could be obtained in singing or with other musical instruments, such as the 'swelling hautboy' mentioned by the anonymous author of the text of Purcell's 1694 birthday song for Queen Mary, 'Come, ye Sons of Art, Away.' This is amply corroborated by Burney's insistence on it, or, rather, by his surprise and indignation at not finding swells in the organs he visited abroad. In his *History of Music*, he remarked that 'next to singing, the most pleasing kinds [of music] are those which approach the nearest to vocal; such as can be sustained, swelled, and diminished, at pleasure. Of these, the first in rank are such as the most excellent performers produce from the Violin, Flute, and Hautbois' (*History*, I, 22). Consequently, it was crucial for the organ to be able to achieve the same effects as these instruments. Burney explained:

> Before I left England, M. Snetzler had told me, that I should doubtless find *swells* in Berlin organs, though he was not certain that this improvement, which was English, had been adopted in other places on the continent; for Mr. Handel, several years ago, had desired him to describe, in writing, the

---

[107] Routh, *Early English Organ Music*, 200.

manner in which the swell was produced, that he might send it to a particular
friend in Berlin, who very much wished to introduce it there.

But I enquired in vain of musical people in that city, whether they knew of
any such machine, as a swell, worked by pedals, in any of their organs; no
such contrivance had ever been heard of, and it was difficult to explain it.
(*Music in Germany*, I, 103–4)

Even though the first written indication of swelling on a printed score was
only to be found around 1760 (in Voluntary No. 6 in D minor in William
Walond's third set of voluntaries), there is no doubt that organists would use
the swell pedal as a matter of course. The importance of swelling was duly
mentioned by John Marsh:

First, it should be considered that no Music can be expressive that is not
accented, marked, or enforced at proper intervals, as at the Beginning, and
sometimes (in common time) in the middle of a bar. This may be in a great
measure effected on the Swell of the organ, by the management of the pedal,
especially in Slow Movements, (which are most proper for the Swell) but on
the other parts of the organ, must be done by other means, such as
Appoggiaturas, and by occasionally doubling the Bass note at the accented
parts, by taking the Octave.[108]

John Marsh further explained the practical use of the swell, which 'can be used
in accompanying Voices instead of the Treble of the Choir Organ, for which it
may be sometimes more convenient, as the Sound may be increased or diminished so as to accommodate such Voices as may require such assistance'.[109]
However, the swell must have been used primarily in voluntaries, especially
when using the Hautboy stop, so that the melody should be as expressive as
possible, in imitation of a singing voice or solo instrument.

The scarcity of precise indications about the way the swell pedal was used
should not come as a surprise. Very often, a stylistic mannerism shared by all the
performers of the same school in a given country and period is so obvious to
them, so 'natural', as it were, that it barely requires explanation. A case in point
is the question of *notes inégales* in French baroque music, which is as crucial to
its performance as seemingly elusive in the score. The practice was so deeply
ingrained in the training of musicians that it was useless to mention it.
Conversely, there were sometimes mentions of places where notes were to be
played strictly as written, without inequality, which is a clear indication that this
was not the norm.[110] Similarly, it is interesting to note William Russell's
specific instruction *not* to use the swell pedal in the second movement of

---

[108] Marsh, 'Preface', *Eighteen Voluntaries*, v.   [109] Marsh, 'Preface', *Eighteen Voluntaries*, iv.
[110] See David Ponsford, *French Organ Music in the Reign of Louis XIV* (Cambridge: Cambridge
University Press, 2011), 51.

Voluntary No. 4 in his second book (1812): the Swell Cornet is to be used in this instance as a mere echo to the Great Cornet and not as an expressive stop. Here, Russell is primarily interested in the contrast in volume between the two manuals using the same registration and tone colour. Another reason that may have prompted Russell to write this down precisely is the fact that the swell pedal was not always used very appropriately by organists. This can be clearly seen in John Marsh's advice to organists:

> As to the peculiar advantage and effect of the Swell in expressing the Pianos, Fortes, Crescendos, and Diminuendos, the performer must there be left to his own judgment, as no particular rules can be given in extempore performance. He should however consider that the mere see-sawing the Pedal up and down at random, and without meaning, can have no better effect than what is produced by a peal of Bells ringing on a windy day.[111]

The organist's 'judgment' – that is, his own good taste – was the ultimate arbiter of a good use of the swell pedal, which is probably why the scores are sparing of indications on how to use it. Jonas Blewitt gave the same recommendation as Marsh: 'the Swell, however, is frequently treated in an improper manner, namely, by moving the foot too hastily up and down: in fact, it should be used only by the slowest gradation, particularly in a full Swell piece'.[112]

Beyond the question of the swell, Burney was also critical of the fact that, in these large continental instruments, the addition of unisons and octaves did not allow for changes of colour. Repeatedly, in outlining his own conception of what a good organ ought to be like, he insisted upon the importance of variety, the latter being produced by the solo stops at the organist's disposal. His visit to the celebrated Müller organ at St Bavo in Haarlem is particularly significant in this respect. This organ had been built by Johann Christian Müller (1690–1763), a Dutch organ builder of German origin, who had taken over the workshop of Cornelis Hoornbeeck in Amsterdam at the latter's death in 1722. It was a monumental three-manual organ, the largest organ in the world at the time of its completion, with over sixty stops and thirty-two-feet pedal-towers. It had been erected between 1735 and 1738 and was to be played by several famous musicians, such as Handel, the young Mozart (in April 1766, when he was still only ten year's old[113]) and, later, Felix Mendelssohn. This famous organ was long considered to be the most impressive instrument in Europe and became emblematic for the Hill-

---

[111] Marsh, 'Preface', *Eighteen Voluntaries*, vii–viii.

[112] Jonas Blewitt, *Complete Treatise on the Organ* (London: Longman and Broderip, 1794), 4. See Philip Sawyer, 'A Neglected Late 18th Century Organ Treatise', *B.I.O.S. Journal*, no. 10 (1986), 80.

[113] See Leopold Mozart, 'Letter to Lorenz Hagenauer, 16 May 1766', in *The Letters of Mozart and His Family*, ed. Emily Anderson (London: Macmillan Press, 1966), 65.

Gauntlett generation of organists and organ builders, on account of the sublime effects it could produce.[114] However, although Burney's expectation was very high, he was 'somewhat disappointed' and criticised the organ for its lack of variety in spite of its 60-odd stops, the poor imitative quality of its Vox Humana, its excessive noise and heavy touch (*Music in Germany*, 304–5). It is quite characteristic that he should have expressed some disappointment concerning this organ, as though he made a point of not yielding blindly to the generally shared opinion. By not endorsing the common assumption about the Müller organ, Burney actually justified the reason for his journey around Europe: it is only by visiting places, and listening to the musicians and hearing the organs in those places, that it is possible for one to forge a valid, unbiased opinion, not by repeating comments or confirming judgements handed over by other travellers. Significantly, in his *History of Music*, he was later to rectify some of his original statements in *The Present State of Music in Germany*. These, he asserted, had resulted from 'the opinion of another person', which he now disowned; he was 'now more than ever convinced, that this opinion, which accused Germany of want of genius, was unjust, and founded on prejudice and ignorance of Teutonic discoveries and atchievements [*sic*] in the whole circle of arts and sciences' (*History* II, 963).

Further, it is interesting that Burney should not mention the power and sublimity of the Haarlem instrument, which was what most visitors would generally comment upon. Not particularly drawn to the loudness of the full organ, Burney preferred to turn his attention to one particular stop, the Vox Humana, which was often praised for its beauty. For him, such a stop should properly imitate the human voice, and he repeatedly assessed Vox Humanas specifically in terms of their imitative quality. For example, he found the Vox Humana of the organ of St Peter's Church in Hamburg 'excellent' but remarked that, 'though not like a human voice, [it] resembles, in tone and in sweetness, a better kind of clarinet' (*Music in Germany*, II, 278). In St Martin's Church, the Vox Humana 'is very sweet, but resembles a fine hautbois or clarinet, more than a human voice' (*Music in Germany*, II, 282–83). In the Dominicans' church in Frankfurt, he found the organ 'better toned, and more in tune than the rest, but it was not so good as many [he had] heard in England, nor was the *Vox Humana* remarkably sweet, or like the human voice, though it [was] much admired here' (*Music in Germany*, I, 77). Even the Vox Humana of the Silbermann organ in the Elector's Chapel at Dresden failed to please Burney, who thought it was 'bad' and found 'there [were] very few solo stops that [were] agreeable' in that organ (*Music in Germany*, II, 56). Only one such stop found favour in his eyes – that

---

[114] Nicholas Thistlethwaite, *The Making of the Victorian Organ* (Cambridge: Cambridge University Press, 1990), 210.

of the organ in the New Church in Amsterdam, which he deemed was 'one of the best stops, of that kind, which [he had] ever heard' (*Music in Germany*, II, 298-99). Thus, the Vox Humana seems to have had a particular significance for him, as though that stop was the ultimate test of the ability of the organ builder to make a sweet, imitative solo stop. As we have seen, artists were advised to take their cues from Nature, so it was logical that the imitation of the most natural of all musical 'instruments', the human voice, should be deemed essential.

Like all organists, Burney was obviously interested in the technical aspect of the instruments he visited. In his *History*, he manifested his fascination for the complexity of the organ as a mechanism: 'An organ is so operose, complicated, and comprehensive a piece of mechanism, that to render it complete in tone, touch, variety, and power, exclusive of the external beauty and majesty of its form and appearance, is perhaps one of the greatest efforts of human ingenuity and contrivance' (*History* II, 343–4). It is interesting, incidentally, that, in his description of the band of musicians and singers at the Handel Commemoration, he should reciprocally have resorted to a mechanical metaphor, mentioning 'all the wheels of that huge machine, the Orchestra', the effect of which, once they were set in motion, 'resembled clock-work in every thing, but want of feeling and expression' (*Account*, 15). This reveals his fascination for the fact that a complex mechanical contraption should be able to trigger emotions. Whenever he saw an instrument of particular interest, whether on account of its sheer size, or because it had been erected by a famous organ builder, he made it a point to give a detailed description of the aspects that had struck him most. Such descriptions are not very numerous in the two books of travels, but they reveal Burney's good understanding of the art of organ building, as well as his curiosity towards whatever disposition he had not previously encountered. However, he sometimes struggled to understand the character and role of some stops, and even the transcription of the spelling of their names is not always consistent. Thus, in Frankfurt,

> the labels of some stops excited my curiosity; such as the *Posaun*, *Salicional*, *Cymbel*, *Suavial*, *Violon*, &c. in the great organ; and in the choir organ, the *Grosdeduct*, *Kleingedukt*, *Violdgamba*, &c., but, being out of order, they were totally unfit to be played, as solo stops. I could just discover that the *Suavial* was meant for that sweet stop in Mr. Snetzler's organs, which he calls the *Dulcian*; and the *Violon*, for the *Violone*, or double base; it is a half stop, which goes no higher than the middle C. (*Music in Germany*, I, 76)

Burney also paid attention to the most remarkable organ cases, such as that in Cologne Cathedral (then unfinished), with its 'three complete and elegant buffets' (*Music in Germany*, I, 70). In Vienna, he visited the beautiful organ erected by Johann David Sieber in the Michaelerkirche in 1714 (a church associated with Haydn and Mozart, whose Requiem was probably first performed there at least in part in 1791). The organ consisted of two identical separated cases on either side of the west window and a *Rückpositiv* located in the middle of the loft. There was also a continuo section integrated in the free-standing console, like that of the Weingarten organ illustrated in Dom Bedos's treatise: 'the instrument has no front, the great pipes are placed, in an elegant manner, on each side of the gallery, and there is a box only in the middle, of about four feet square, for the keys and stops; so that the west window is left quite open' (*Music in Germany*, II, 276–7).

Burney was eager to hear and examine organs built by the better-known and most celebrated organ builders on the continent. He paid particular attention to 'old' Gottfried Silbermann's organ in the Frauenkirche, Dresden, a large thirty-two -foot instrument of forty-eight stops on three manuals and pedals. As usual, Burney was critical of the touch, which was 'so heavy, that each key requires a foot, instead of a finger, to press it down'. And he regretted that the reed stops should be 'but seven in number, so that the imitations and changes are very few'. He was more interested in the solo stops than in the plenum, and he listed the best ones, namely the Viol da Gamba, Bassoon, Vox Humana, Trumpet, Schalmo, Tremulant and *Schwebung*, which imitates a close shake. To conclude, Burney explained that, this being the first instrument by Silbermann he had visited, he 'entered inside the case, and found the work strong, neat, and well-disposed: it is remarkable that to so immense a machine, there are but five bellows' (*Music in Germany*, III, 48–9).

In Alost, in Flanders, he visited the church of St Martin and saw its new, 'noble' organ built by Van Petigham & Son of Ghent: 'Its form is elegant, and the ornaments are in good taste. It has fifty-three stops, three sets of keys, great organ, choir organ and echo, down to bottom F, on the fourth line in the base'. He was surprised that the touch should not be 'so heavy as might be expected from the great resistance of such a column of air as is necessary for so considerable a number of stops'. He found the reed stops 'well-toned', the Diapasons 'well-voiced' and the Chorus 'rich and noble'. He concluded that 'the French organ-builders are much esteemed by the Germans themselves, for the simplification of their movements, and the mechanism of the whole; but the variety which these stops afford is not proportioned to their number; we have frequently more solo stops in an English organ of half the size and price' (*Music in Germany*, I, 20–1).

7 National Pride

Burney was generally rather critical in his assessment of continental organs. Although he would occasionally admit that a particular organ was well voiced or worked well, he seems to have been dissatisfied with the general aesthetic philosophy or outlook that presided over the art of organ building abroad. The smaller, more restrained English organ with its expressive solo stops, swell mechanism and subtle action seemed to him to be a better vehicle for the performance of refined and elegant music. While he was curious and seemed genuinely open to the musical culture of European countries, Burney nonetheless voiced a feeling of national pride in the superiority of British taste in music and the art of organ building.[115] His distaste for large and loud organs with heavy actions and useless, cumbersome pedals; his frequent annoyance at noisy accompaniments and large, resonant buildings where all was confusion; his impression that organs abroad were often out of tune and organists not always competent enough; his disapproval of organ music that was either too light and lacking in dignity, or too laboured and artificial – all these various impressions amount *a contrario* to a plea in favour of British taste, and a proud advocacy of the English organ as Burney knew it. Travelling abroad was for Burney a way of asserting the superiority of Britain in matters aesthetic, as well as the quality of English craftsmen. That superiority of national art, which, aesthetically speaking, was founded upon a dialectic of moderation and sublimity, went hand in hand with a criticism of continental art, which was considered unnatural. This could paradoxically be called an attitude of 'insular cosmopolitanism', to use Jeremy Black's humorous phrase,[116] that is, a manner of finding in foreign culture some *a contrario* confirmation of the superiority of one's own values, as John Villiers expressed clearly in 1789: 'We know not the value of our privileges ... till we have felt the loss of them, and every young man ought to go abroad, to make him the more attached to his own country. I find everything here so extremely inferior, that I glow with pride and rapture, when I think I am an Englishman.'[117]

According to Burney, organ building had reached a degree of excellence in Britain that was far superior to the productions of continental organ builders. Mechanically, English organs were less noisy and more comfortable to play:

> The *touch* too of the organ, which our builders have so much improved, still remains in its heavy, noisy state. And now I am on this subject, I must observe, that most of the organs which I met with on the Continent, seem to be inferior to ours built by father Smith, Byfield, or Snetzler, in everything but size. As the churches there are often immense, so are the organs; the tone is indeed somewhat softened and refined by space and distance; but when heard

---

[115] See Pierre Dubois, 'The 18th c. English Organ and the Collective Psyche: a Vehicle for National Ideals', *B.I.O.S Journal*, no. 20, 100–115.

[116] Lecture given at the annual Conference of the *Société d'Études Anglo-Américaines des XVIIe et XVIIIe Siècles*, La Sorbonne, Paris, 25 November 1995.

[117] John C. Villiers, *A Tour through Part of France, Containing a Description of Paris, Cherbourg, and Ermenonville, with a Rhapsody Composed at the Tomb of Rousseau; in a Series of Letters* (London: T. Cadell, 1789), 33.

near, it is intolerably coarse and noisy; and though the number of stops in these large instruments is very great, they afford but little variety, being, for the most part, duplicates in unisons and octaves to each other, such as the great and small 12ths, flutes, and 15ths: hence in our organs not only the touch and tone, but the imitative stops are greatly superior to those of any other organs that I have met with. (*Music in Germany*, 299)[118]

The very vocabulary used by Burney in this passage is particularly interesting: British organ builders are described, and hailed, as the upholders of modern art, which is considered as superior to former usages ('*improved*'); this modern art is characterised by good taste and pleasant effects which are opposed to the 'coarseness' of foreign organs; 'variety' is defined as one of the foremost values that should be propounded, as it is by English organ builders; and it is because the latter know well how to build 'imitative stops' that they are superior to the foreign builders. English organs, which were smaller and less powerful, generally had a lighter action, which Burney considered a prerequisite for a good instrument:

The touch of the keys should be free and elastic, and exactly the same pressure should be requisite to put down every key throughout the scale. No better proof can be given of a good touch, than that a turned shake can be executed with equal facility in every part of the scale, except perhaps in the lowest octave, where it is not expected or desired. If all these things act without noise, the mechanical parts of the organ may be considered good, and in order. (*Music in France*, 390)

In Rees's *Cyclopedia*, Burney linked the superior quality of English instruments to the social context and conditions under which these were built. Though he acknowledged that the best keyed instruments in England had been built by craftsmen of German origin, he explained that the workmanship was better in Britain because workers were better paid than abroad:

The organs in our churches, that have been well preserved of father Schmidt's make, such as St Paul's, the Temple, St Mary's, Oxford, Trinity college, Cambridge, &c. are far superior in tone to any of more modern construction; but the mechanism has been improved during the last century, by Byfield, Snetzler, Green, Gray, etc. The touch is lighter, the compass extended, and the reed-work admirable. The dulciana stop, brought hither by Snetzler, is a tall, delicate, narrow pipe, of an exquisite sweet tone, without a reed; on which account it stands in tune equally well with the open diapason. Though the best keyed-instruments in England have been made by Germans, they work here better than in their own country in size and number of stops; they greatly surpass us in the size of their organs, but

---

[118] See also *Music in Germany* 13, 164, 220.

the mechanism is infinitely inferior; which is accounted for by the work-manship being better paid here than in the German dominions, where labour is cheap. (*Cyclopedia*, vol. 25, n.p.)

By this deft sleight of hand, Burney re-appropriated German-born organ builders and conferred their success on his own country. It was only in England that these foreign craftsmen were able to bring their art to the highest level of excellence, which they owed to the improved social and economic circumstances made possible by English society. The praise of English organ builders implied praise of the political, social and economic system of the British nation.

Burney had used the same 'nationalising' device concerning Handel in his *Account of the ... Commemoration of Handel*, which he wrote at the King's request in 1785. We have already seen that he considered Handel the best organist in Europe. He wrote that Handel's compositions for the organ and harpsichord, with those of Scarlatti and Alberti, 'were [his] chief practise and delight, for more than fifty years' (*History*, II, 510), and that 'Handel's organ concertos long remained in possession of the first and favourite places, in the private practice and public performance of every organist in the kingdom' (*History*, II, 1008). In his *Account of the Commemoration*, he paid a tribute to the 'national' composer Handel had become and attempted to identify him with the spirit of the British nation:

> Handel, whose genius and abilities have lately been so noble commemorated, though not a native of England, spent the greatest part of his life in the service of its inhabitants: improving our taste, delighting us in the church, the theatre, and the chamber; and introducing among us so many species of musical excellence, that, during more than half a century, while sentiment, not fashion, guided our applause, we neither wanted nor wished for any other standard. He arrived among us at a barbarous period for almost every kind of music, except that of the church. ... Indeed his works were so long the models of perfection in this country, that they may be said to have formed our national taste. For though many in the capital have been partial, of late years, to the compositions of Italy, Germany, and France; yet the nation at large has rather tolerated than adopted these novelties.
>
> The English, a manly, military race, were instantly captivated by the grave, bold, and nervous style of Handel, which is congenial with their manners and sentiments. (*Account*, pp. iii–iv)

Burney's reasoning was circular: although Handel was born in Germany, he is shown to have been perfectly at one with the 'manly' character of the British people, so that his ability to 'fashion the national taste' of his adopted country reciprocally confirmed that his style was 'congenial' with the manners of the 'Britons'. Implicitly, it is suggested that in no other country would Handel have been able to develop the same *œuvre*, which was so intrinsically bound up with the native genius of the country. This constitutes the backbone to the Commemoration of Handel, which binds together the glorification of the dead composer, the Church and the State, and the united English people, symbolically represented by the audience, choir and orchestra gathered around the Green organ in Westminster Abbey, under the authority of King George III, as illustrated in the painting by Edward Edwards reproduced in Burney's *Account* (Figure 12).

In private, Burney conceded that he was 'drawn off from the exclusive wrship [of Handel, Corelli and Scarlatti] before [he] was 20, by keeping company with travelled & heterodox gentlemen, who were partial to the Music of more modern composers whom they had heard in Italy' (*Letters*, to Thomas Twining, 14 Dec. 1781 and 31 July 1784). He thought that Joah Bates (the conductor at the Commemoration) and King George III were excessively fond of Handel and declared that he, Burney, refused to 'abuse the lovers of the best Music of Italy & Germany' by saying that 'there is no other Music fit to be heard, or as well performed'. By then, Burney had discovered the music of Haydn, in particular, and fully embraced it. In spite of his genuine admiration for Handel, he refused to place him alone on a pedestal. Nonetheless, his adherence to the virtues of his native country was sincere, and, as we have seen, he saw in the English organ a particularly fit expression of these virtues.

8 Sociability, Manners and Politeness

In the 'Preface' to his *History of Music*, Burney based the significance of music on the universality of its appeal.[119] He saw music as a form of art that was beneficial to the public good. The book is therefore much more than a mere 'history'. In all history of music, there is a 'view of society ..., a view of humanity'.[120] What mattered to Burney as much as writing a compendium of factual or historical information was the notion that sympathy (or 'fellow-feeling', as Adam Smith also called it in his *Theory of Moral Sentiments*[121]) and sociability were part and parcel of the broad notion of taste. 'Manners', declared Burke, 'are of more importance than laws ... they aid morals, they supply them, or they totally destroy them.'[122] The test of taste lay in a global conception of politeness as

---

[119] K. C. Balderston, 'Dr Johnson and Burney's *History of Music*', *PMLA*, vol. 49, no. 3 (Sep. 1934), 966–8 (968),www.jstor.org/stable/458395.

[120] Green, 'The Impact of Rousseau', 6.

[121] Adam Smith, *The Theory of Moral Sentiments* (London: Andrew Millar, and Edinburgh: Alexander Kincaid and J. Bell, 1759), *passim*.

[122] Edmund Burke, *Letters on a Regicide Peace*, 1796 (*The Works of the Right Honorable Edmund Burke*, London: F. C. and J. Rivington, 1826, vol. VIII, p. 172), quoted in J. G. A. Pocock, 'Virtues, Rights, and Manners: A Model for Historians of Political Thought', in *Political Theory*, vol. 9, no. 3 (Aug. 1981), 353–68.www.jstor.org/stable/191094, 366.

Figure 12 *The Handel Commemoration at Westminster*, 1784, by Edward Edwards. Charles Burney, *An Account of the musical Performances in Westminster Abbey and the Pantheon (May 26th, 27th, 29th; and June the 3rd, and 5th, 1784) in Commemoration of Handel* (London: G. Robinson, 1785), pl. VII

a form of virtue. For, as Pocock has shown, virtue was redefined in the eighteenth century 'with the aid of the concept of manners' as the new individual 'moved from the farmer-warrior model of citizenship' and 'entered an increasingly transactional universe of "commerce and the arts"'.[123] The notion of politeness and the practice of sociability were grounded in the theory of sympathy. According to Adam Smith, sympathy contributed to the creation of the social order and the moderation of the individual passions. Consequently, sociability and politeness occupied a central place in eighteenth-century Britain. As Lawrence E. Klein explains, 'politeness', which was 'one of the myths of the age', can be taken as an 'analytical category', since it 'informed cultural practice'.[124] The language of politeness became a 'major fixture of English discourse' from the early eighteenth century, and was represented in an array of key words (such as 'refinement', 'manners', 'breeding', 'civility', etc.) and a range of qualifying attributes ('free', 'easy', 'natural', graceful', etc.).[125] 'The language of politeness had enormous power in its day', Paul Langford remarks.[126]

Tellingly, in a conversation with Mrs. Thrale (reported by Frances Burney), Dr Johnson praised Burney as 'a man for everybody to love. It is but natural to love him – I question if there be in the world such another man altogether for mind, intelligence, and *manners* [my italics] as Dr Burney.'[127] Manners, we understand, were of paramount importance in assessing the moral worth and character of a person. Burney's conception of the organ was predicated on the importance of manners and politeness. This applied both to the instrument and its practitioners. It is clearly perceptible in Burney's comments on the organs and organists he encountered during his two tours of the continent.

First, he considered moderation a distinctive sign of politeness. His rejection of 'coarse' instruments, loud stops and noisy actions was more than an aesthetic appreciation. It implied an ethical judgement. We witnessed the impression left on him by the spectacle of Mr Binder who, after playing on the stiff manuals and using the pedals, was 'in as violent a heat with fatigue and exertion, as if he had run eight or ten miles, full-speed, over ploughed lands in the dog-days' (quoted above, *Music in Germany*, 147–8). For Burney, such musical practice was clearly lacking in refinement and decorum.

Secondly, Burney's constant plea for musical simplicity and moderation, his rejection of laboured compositions or excessively crowded accompaniments

---

[123] Pocock, 'Virtues, Rights and Manners', 365.

[124] Lawrence E. Klein, 'Politeness and the Interpretation of the British Eighteenth Century', *The Historical Journal*, vol. 45, no.4 (2002), 869–98, www.jstor.org/stable/3133532, 870.

[125] Lawrence E. Klein, 'Liberty, Manners and Politeness in Early Eighteenth-Century England', vol. 32, no. 3 (1989), 583–605. See also Paul Langford, 'The Uses of Eighteenth-Century Politeness', *Transactions of the Royal Historical Society*, vol. 12 (2002), 311–31, www.jstor.org/stable/3679350, 311–12.

[126] Langford, 'The Uses of Eighteenth-Century Politeness', 315.

[127] Frances Burney, *Memoirs of Doctor Burney*, vol. II, 176.

and his distaste of loudness as well as of intricacy are all linked to an ethos of politeness and restraint. He thought that pedantry, excessive sophistication and affectation were moral vices. As William Weber has remarked, eighteenth-century music evinced a 'sense of propriety that abhorred speaking in excessively serious terms'.[128] A pompous and stilted style was frowned upon and *galant* musical aesthetics favoured 'a self-conscious discursive style, full of qualification and relativism, [that was] apt to find the funny side of things',[129] not unlike, it could be argued, what Laurence Sterne's novels (*The Life and Opinions of Tristram Shandy* and *A Sentimental Journey*) brilliantly achieved in the sphere of literature.[130] The musical style itself was supposed to express forms of sociability through its inner dialogical organisation and the avoidance of abstruse, unpalatable elaboration.[131]

Thirdly, Burney was particularly attentive to the politeness of the organists and musicians he met. When he visited Balbastre in Paris, he was delighted with the French organist's civility and warm welcome. Balbastre was friendly, hospitable and well mannered. Even though he was not expected at St-Roch that day, he went there on purpose to meet Burney (*Music in France*, 37). After showing all the aspects of his talent on the organ, the French organist invited Burney to his own apartment and played for him again on his Ruckers harpsichord. In his travel notebook, Burney explained that there was a company of twelve to fourteen ladies and nearly as many gentlemen, and he gave the following description:

> En verité says one of the ladies who had been at church M. Balbastre vous etes ravissans [*sic*]. He played a great deal and soon found out by my talk, and approbation that I was a performer he pressed me very much to play and as he had been so obliging himself I sat down at the harpsichord with as little fuss as my great want of practice required. French politeness was not wanting tho' I had not much partiality for myself. However this was a useful and agreeable visit. (*Music, Men, and Manners*, 17)

The scene depicted is a perfect illustration of polite and genteel eighteenth-century society in which mutual sympathy or fellow-feeling plays a crucial role.

---

[128] William Weber, 'Did People Listen in the 18th Century?', *Early Music*, no. 25 (1997), 678–91, 683.

[129] W. Dean Sutcliffe, 'The Shapes of Sociability in the Instrumental Music of the Later Eighteenth Century', *Journal of the Royal Musical Association*, vol. 138, no. 1, 1–45, DOI: https://doi.org /10.1080/02690403.2013.771941.

[130] Interestingly, Mark Evan Bonds has likened Sterne's wit and humour to aspects of Haydn's style. See Mark Evan Bonds, 'Haydn, Laurence Sterne, and the Origins of Musical Irony', *Journal of the American Musicological Society*, vol. 44, no. 1 (Spring, 1991), 57–91.

[131] See W. Dean Sutcliffe, *Instrumental Music in an Age of Sociability: Haydn, Mozart and Friends* (Cambridge: Cambridge University Press, 2019), *passim*.

Burney's description of Balbastre's courtesy, and his desire to please his foreign visitor and make his visit both instructive and pleasant, paints a portrait of a refined and delicate man who is attentive to others. And his manner of playing pertains to this social refinement. The lady's exclamation, 'en verité ... Mr. Balbastre vous etes ravissans' [*sic*] ('you are ravishing') sums up better than any detailed description what constituted Balbastre's charm in the eyes of his contemporaries, for, as the Littré dictionary explains, a ravishing or delightful man was someone who could make himself agreeable in society. Beyond this, Balbastre was able to delight and 'ravish' his listeners through his musical talent, that is, to allow them to escape for a while from their present contingency through aesthetic emotion. Balbastre's pleasing sociability accorded with the delicacy of his music. He delighted his listeners because his performance and his politeness were in harmony with one another and corresponded to the prevailing social codes in his milieu. As Alain Viala has remarked, 'sociability aims at approval [*agrément*]: one must be agreeable to be approved ... What matters is to please others, or "the other"'.[132]

That same civility was corroborated during the meeting between Burney, Balbastre and A.-L. Couperin at St-Gervais the following day. Burney explained that he was happy to see 'two eminent men of the same profession, so candid and friendly together' (*Music in France*, 41). Social and musical harmony go hand in hand, which corresponds to the ideal of the age of Enlightenment as expressed by James Beattie, who connected sympathy and music in his *Essay on Poetry and Music as They Affect the Mind*; and which was well summed up by Charles Avison in his *Essay on Musical Expression*, when he explained that 'it [was] the peculiar Quality of Music to raise the *Sociable and happy Passions*, and to *subdue* the *contrary ones*' and that the passions raised by music were 'of the benevolent and social Kind, and in their Intent at least [were] disinterested and noble'.[133] In the same way, Burney commented on his visit to Balbastre that he was 'satisfied both with his performance and politeness' (*Music in France*, 40). The musician's moral qualities are at one with his professional and artistic abilities. Burney thus binds together the good and the beautiful, following a philosophical tradition going back to Lord Shaftesbury. Ethics and aesthetics are closely intertwined. Similarly, in his

---

[132] Alain Viala, *La galanterie: une mythologie française* (Paris: Éditions du Seuil, 2019), 371.

[133] Charles Avison, *An Essay on Musical Expression* (London: C. Davis, 1752–3), ed. Dubois, *Charles Avison's Essay on Musical Expression and Related Writings by Charles Avison and William Hayes* (Aldershot: Ashgate, 2004), 6. See also Pierre Dubois, '"Music ... Is Like a Conversation Among Friends Where the Few Are of One Mind": *Charles Avison's Moral Philosophy*', in *Charles Avison in Context: National and International Musical Links in Eighteenth-Century North-East England*, ed. Roz Southey and Eric Cross (Aldershot: Ashgate, 2017), 1–17, *passim*.

Memoirs of the life and writings of the Abate Metastasio, Burney wrote: 'But this poet has still higher claims on our reverence and affection, from his innoxious life and moral character, which give a kind of dignity to innocent pleasure, and to humanity.'[134] For Burney, taste was intrinsically bound up with the notion of sympathy and the connection between human beings. Taste has a civilising impact and, in order to prove tasteful, one must be harmoniously connected with others.[135]

*

As Peter Williams once remarked, the subject of the English organ before 1800 is 'one of comparatively minor interest from an international point of view since few if any of its builders have ever had an influence outside Britain and its Empire, despite some outstanding successes at home'.[136] Overshadowed notably by the great organ compositions of Johann Sebastian Bach, the English repertory of the eighteenth century is generally rated as frivolous, technically mediocre or second-rate, and the function of the organ in England is reduced to its role as that of an instrument mainly used for the purposes of accompaniment. The organ, however, fulfilled a number of important functions in Georgian society, both inside and outside the Church (oratorios, organ concertos, pleasure gardens, chamber organs), and it may be misleading to appraise it according to erroneous criteria borrowed from other cultural traditions. Contrary to the generally accepted view according to which the small size, overall sweetness and restrained character of English organs were evidence of the poverty of the English school of organ building, it may be argued that these characteristics were deliberate and purposeful, not only in terms of the roles imparted to the organ, but also in relation to distinctive criteria of taste and a coherent set of aesthetic and philosophical notions.

No better introduction to the aesthetic ethos of the eighteenth-century English organ can be found than in Charles Burney's remarks disseminated in his various writings. in which he articulated his musical appreciation on a global view of society. He conceived the organ therefore as the locus of ethical as well as aesthetic claims. His conception of the instrument, its repertoire and its users encapsulated, or reflected, his broader outlook on life and human exchanges. Simplicity, sensibility, fancy and moderation, which he believed were the constituents of good taste as well as good manners, were the criteria whereby

---

[134] Charles Burney, *Memoirs of the life and writings of the Abate Metastasio: In which are incorporated, translations of his principal letters* (London: G. G. and J. Robinson, 1796), preface, iii.

[135] Lipking, *The Ordering of the Arts*, 295.

[136] Peter Williams, *A New History of the Organ, from the Greeks to the Present Day* (London & Boston: Faber and Faber, 1980), 131.

he assessed the quality of both organs and organists. He sought in music this 'tranquil pleasure, short of rapture ..., in which intellect and sensation are equally concerned' (*History*, II, 7). It is fascinating to observe the way in which, page after page, Burney consistently hailed the English organ of his time – long disparaged abroad and derided for its idiosyncrasies – as the very epitome of excellence and overall elegance. An admirer of Italian music, the German symphony and the ideas of Rousseau, Burney was open to foreign influences and the modern style of music of his time. Yet when it came to the organ, he abided by the model set by Georgian organ builders and subscribed to the light, versatile, graceful style of the English organists of his time.

Abbreviations Used for Burney's Works Quoted

Account	*An Account of the Musical Performances in Westminster Abbey and the Pantheon in Commemoration of Handel* (1785).
Cyclopedia	'Organ' entry, in Abraham Rees, *The Cyclopedia, or Universal Dictionary of Arts, Sciences and Literature* (1819).
History	*A General History of Music from the Earliest Ages to the Present Period* (1776–89).
Letters	*The Letters of Dr Charles Burney from 1751 to 1784* (1784, ed. Alvaro Ribeiro, S. J. 1991).
Memoirs	*Memoirs of Dr Charles Burney, 1726–1769*, ed. Slava Klima, Garry Bowers and Kerry S. Grant (1984).
Music in France	*The Present State of Music in France and Italy; or, the Journal of a Tour through those Countries undertaken to collect Materials for a General History of Music* (1771–1773).
Music in Germany	*The Present State of Music in Germany, the Netherlands, and United Provinces* (1773).
Music, Men, and Manners	*Music, Men, and Manners in France and Italy, Being the Journal written by Charles Burney, Mus. D., during a Year through those Countries, undertaken to collect material for <u>A General History of Music</u>* (1770, transcription of the original manuscript by H. Edmund Poole, 1969).

Bibliography

Primary Sources

Acts and Ordinances of the Interregnum, 1642–1660, ed. C. H. Firth and R. S. Rait (London, 1911), 425–6, www.british-history.ac.uk/no-series /acts-ordinances-interregnum.

Avison, Charles. *An Essay on Musical Expression*. London: C. Davis, 1752–53, ed. Pierre Dubois, *Charles Avison's Essay on Musical Expression and Related Writings by Charles Avison and William Hayes*. Aldershot: Ashgate, 2004.

Banner, Richard. *The Use and Antiquity of Musick in the Services of God*. Oxford, 1737.

Beattie, James. *Essays on Poetry and Music as They Affect the Mind*. London: E. and C. Dilly and W. Creech, Edinburgh, 1779.

Bedford, Arthur. *The Great Abuse of Musick*. London, 1711.

Blewitt, Jonas. *Complete Treatise on the Organ*. London: Longman and Broderip, 1794.

Burke, Edmund. *A Philosophical Enquiry into the Origin of our Ideas of the Sublime and Beautiful* (1757), ed. Adam Philips. Oxford & New York: Oxford University Press, 1990.

Letters on a Regicide Peace, 1796, in *The Works of the Right Honorable Edmund Burke*. London: F. C. and J. Rivington, 1826.

Burney, Charles. *An Account of the Musical Performances in Westminster Abbey and the Pantheon in Commemoration of Handel*. London: G. Robinson, 1785.

A General History of Music from the Earliest Ages to the Present Period. London: n.p., 1776–89. (republished New York: Dover Publications, 2 vols, 1957).

The Letters of Dr Charles Burney from 1751 to 1784 (1784), ed. S. J. Alvaro Ribeiro. Oxford: Clarendon Press, 1991.

Memoirs of Dr Charles Burney, 1726–1769, ed. Slava Klima, Garry Bowers and Kerry S. Grant. Lincoln and London: University of Nebraska Press, 1984.

Memoirs of the life and writings of the Abate Metastasio: In which are incorporated, translations of his principal letters. London: G. G. and J. Robinson, 1796.

Music, Men, and Manners in France and Italy, Being the Journal written by Charles Burney, Mus. D., during a Year through those Countries, undertaken to collect material for A General History of Music, 1770. Transcription of the original manuscript by H. Edmund Poole. London: The Folio Society, 1969.

'Organ' entry. In Abraham Rees (ed.), *The Cyclopedia, or Universal Dictionary of Arts, Sciences and Literature.* London, 1819.

The Present State of Music in France and Italy; or, the Journal of a Tour through those Countries undertaken to collect Materials for a General History of Music. London: T. Beckett & Co., J. Robson and G. Robinson, 1771–73.

The Present State of Music in Germany, the Netherlands, and United Provinces. London: T. Beckett & Co., J. Robson and G. Robinson, 1773.

Burney, Frances [Mme D'Arblay]. *Memoirs of Dr Burney.* London: Edward Moxon, 1832.

Coningesby, George. *Church Music Vindicated; and the Causes of its Dislikes Enquired into.* London, 1733.

Donaldson, John. *Principles of Taste, or the Elements of Beauty.* Edinburgh: n. p., 1786.

Gerard, Alexander. *An Essay on Taste.* Edinburgh: n.p., 1759 (3rd edition, London: Bell, Creech and Cadell, 1780).

Hawkins, John. *A General History of the Science and Practice of Music.* London, 1776. (republished London: Novello, 1875).

Hayes, William. Letter to *The Gentleman's Magazine*, vol. 35, 1765, 213–14.

Home, Henry. *Elements of Criticism.* London: T. Cadell and G. Robinson, 1761 (6th ed., Edinburgh: J. Bell and W. Creech, 1785).

Leffler, Henry. *Leffler Manuscript* [*c*.1802–16]. Facsimile edition with introduction by Peter Williams. Reigate: British Institute of Organ Studies, 2010.

Locke, John. *An Essay Concerning Human Understanding.* London: Thomas Basset, 1690.

Ludlam, William. Letter to *The Gentleman's Magazine*, vol. 24 December 1772, 562–65

Marsh, John. 'History of my private Life.' In *The John Marsh Journals*, ed. Brian Robins. Stuyvesant, NY: Pendragon Press, 1998.

'Preface.' In *Eighteen Voluntaries for the Organ, Chiefly intended for the Use of Young Practitioners.* London: Preston, 1791.

Mason, William. *Essays, Historical and Critical, on English Church Music.* York, 1795. (republished in *The Works of William Mason*, London: T. Cadell and W. Davies, 1811).

Mozart, Leopold. 'Letter to Lorenz Hagenauer, 16 May 1766.' In *The Letters of Mozart and His Family*, ed. Emily Anderson. London: Macmillan Press, 1966, p. 85.

Pope, Alexander. *Essay on Criticism*. London: W. Lewis, 1711. (republished Oxford: Oxford University Press, 1990)

Richardson, Samuel. *The History of Sir Charles Grandison*. London, 1753, ed. Jocelyn Harris. London: Oxford University Press, 1972.

Smith, Adam. *The Theory of Moral Sentiments*. London and Edinburgh: Andrew Millar and Alexander Kincaid and J. Bell, 1759.

Tillotson, John. *The Works*. London: James, John and Paul Knapton, 1735.

Villiers, John C. *A Tour through Part of France, Containing a Description of Paris, Cherbourg, and Ermenonville, with a Rhapsody Composed at the Tomb of Rousseau; in a Series of Letters*. London: T. Cadell, 1789.

Wolcot, John. *Ode Upon Ode*. London: G. Kearsley and W. Forster, 1787.

Secondary Sources

Balderston, K. C. 'Dr Johnson and Burney's *History of Music.' PMLA*, vol. 49, no. 3 (September 1934), 966–8. www.jstor.org/stable/458395

Barnes, Alan and Martin Renshaw. *The Life and Work of John Snetzler*. Aldershot: Scolar Press, 1994.

Barry, Jonathan. 'Cultural Patronage and the Anglican Crisis: Bristol, c. 1689–1775', in John Walsh, Colin Haydon and Stephen Taylor (eds.), *The Church of England, c.1689–c.1833: From Toleration to Tractarianism*. Cambridge: Cambridge University Press, 1993.

Bell, Ian. 'Elegant Sufficiency.' *Choir and Organ*, vol. 23, no. 5 (September/October 2015), 18–22.

Bicknell, Stephen. 'English Organ-Building 1642–1685.' *B. I. O. S. Journal*, no. 5 (1981), 5–22.

 The History of the English Organ. Cambridge: Cambridge University Press, 1996.

Boeringer, James. *Organa Britannica – Organs in Great Britain 1660–1860*. Lewisburg, PA: Bucknell University Press, 1986, vol. II, 164–6.

Bonds, Mark Evan. 'Haydn, Laurence Sterne, and the Origins of Musical Irony.' *Journal of the American Musicological Society*, vol. 44, no. 1 (Spring 1991), 57–91.

Clutton, Cecil, and Austin Niland. *The British Organ*. London: Eyre Methuen, 1963 (republished 1982).

Cruikshank, Dan. *The Royal Hospital Chelsea – the Place and the People*. London: Third Millennium Publishing, 2004.

Dawe, Donovan. *The Organists of the City of London, 1666–1850: a Record of One-Thousand Organists*. Padstow: Donovan Dawe, 1983.

Dean, Captain C. G. T. 'Dr Burney's Connection with the Royal Hospital, Chelsea.' In *Transactions of the London and Middlesex Archaeological Society*, new series, vol. IX. London: Bishopsgate Institute, 1948.

Dubois, Pierre. 'The 18th c. English Organ and the Collective Psyche: a Vehicle for National Ideals.' *B. I. O. S. Journal*, no. 20 (1996), 100–15.

L'orgue dans la société anglaise au XVIIIème siècle: éthique et esthétique de la modération. Lille: Presses Universitaires du Septentrion, 1997.

'"The Organ and Its Music Vindicated"– a Study of "Music Sermons" in Eighteenth-Century England.' *B. I. O. S. Journal*, no. 31 (2007), 40–64.

'The Socio-Cultural Semiotics of Handel's Organ Concertos.' *B. I. O. S. Journal*, no. 34 (2010), 68–81.

Music in the Georgian Novel. Cambridge: Cambridge University Press, 2015.

'Generic Hybridization of the Organ Voluntary, from Henry Purcell to William Russell.' In *Palette pour Marie-Madeleine Martinet*. www .csti.paris-sorbonne.fr/centre/palette/txt/duboisMMMthesesHDR03 .pdf, 2016.

'"Music . . . Is Like a Conversation Among Friends Where the Few Are of One Mind": Charles Avison's Moral Philosophy.' In Roz Southey and Eric Cross (eds.), *Charles Avison in Context: National and International Musical Links in Eighteenth-Century North-East England.* Aldershot, Ashgate, 2017, pp. 1–17.

F. G. E. 'Dr Charles Burney (1726–1814). A Biographical Sketch (Concluded).' *The Musical Times*, vol. 45, no. 739 (1 September 1904), 575–80. www.jstor.org /stable/i237483.

Gorton, John. *A Topographical Dictionary of Great Britain and Ireland.* London: Chapman and Hall, 1833.

Goulden, Colin. *The Organs of All Souls Church, Langham Place, London, and St Peter's Church, Vere Street, London.* London: All Soul's Church, 1976.

Green, Edward. 'The Impact of Rousseau on the *Histories* of Burney and Hawkins: A Study in the Ethics of Musicology.' In *Music's Intellectual History.* New York: RILM, 2009.

Gwynn, Dominic. 'The Origins of the English Style in Church Organ-Building.' *B.I.O.S. Journal*, no. 30 (2006), 116–30.

Harper, John. 'An Organ for St Teilo: a Welsh Instrument in the Pre-Reformation Tradition.' *B.I.O.S. Journal*, no. 35, 134–53.

Hopkins, Edward J. and F. Rimbault. *The Organ, its History and Construction; a Comprehensive Treatise on the Structure and Capabilities of the Organ.* London: Robert Cocks and Co., 1855. (3rd ed. 1877).

Kassler, Michael. 'The English Translations of Forkel's Life of Bach.' In *The English Bach Awakening*, ed. Michael Kassler. Abingdon: Ashgate Publishing/ Routledge, 2004 (republished 2016), 169–210.

Klein, Lawrence E. 'Liberty, Manners and Politeness in Early Eighteenth-Century England.' *The Historical Journal*, vol. 32, no. 3 (1989), 583–605.

'Politeness and the Interpretation of the British Eighteenth Century.' *The Historical Journal*, vol. 45, no. 4 (2002), 869–98. www.jstor.org/stable/ 3133532.

Knight, David S. 'The Battle of the Organs, the Smith Organ at the Temple and its Organist.' *B.I.O.S. Journal*, no. 21(1997), 76–99.

'The Organs of Westminster Abbey and Their Music, 1240–1908', PhD, Historical Musicology (King's College, University of London, 2001).

Langford, Paul. *A Polite and Commercial People – England 1727–1783*. Oxford: Oxford University Press, 1992.

'The Uses of Eighteenth-Century Politeness.' *Transactions of the Royal Historical Society*, vol. 12 (2002), 311–31. www.jstor.org/stable/ 3679350.

Linley, Mark and William Drake. 'Grosvenor Chapel and the 18th-Century Organ.' *B.I.O.S. Journal*, no. 15 (1991), 90–117.

Lipking, Lawrence. *The Ordering of the Arts in Eighteenth-Century England*. Princeton, New Jersey: Princeton University Press, 1970.

Lonsdale, Roger. *Dr Charles Burney, a Literary Biography*. Oxford: The Clarendon Press, 1965.

Luckner, Brian William. 'The Organ Voluntaries of John Stanley.' Doctoral thesis, University of Cincinnati, 1992 (reproduced by University Microfilms International, Ann Arbor, MI).

McCrea, Andrew. 'Introduction.'*Charles Burney Six Cornet Pieces*. Stratford-upon-Avon: Royal College of Organists, March 2015.

Pearce, Charles W. *Notes on English Organs of the Period 1800–1810*. London: The Vincent Music Company Ltd, 1912.

Platt, Richard. 'Plagiarism or Emulation: the Gerard Smith Organ Contract for St George's Church, Hanover Square.' *BIOS Journal*, no. 17 (1997), 32–46.

Plumley, Nicholas M. *The Organs of the City of London*. Oxford: Positif Press, 1996.

Pocock, J. G. A. 'Virtues, Rights, and Manners: A Model for Historians of Political Thought.' *Political Theory*, vol. 9, no. 3 (Aug. 1981), 353–68. www.jstor.org/stable/191094.

Ponsford, David. *French Organ Music in the Reign of Louis XIV.* Cambridge: Cambridge University Press, 2011.

Rasch, Rudolf A. *The New Grove Dictionary of Music and Musicians* (2nd ed.), ed. Stanley Sadie. London: Macmillan Publishers, 2001, vol. 20, pp. 219–20.

Routh, Francis. *Early English Organ Music.* New York: Harper & Row Publishers, Inc., 1973.

Rowntree, John. 'Bernard Smith (c. 1629–1708) Organist and Organbuilder: His Origins.' *B.I.O.S. Journal*, no. 2 (1978), 10–23.

Rumbold, Valerie. 'Music Aspires to Letters: Charles Burney, Queeney Thrale and the Streatham Circle.' *Music & Letters*, vol. 74, no. 1 (Feb. 1993), 24–38.

Sawyer, Philip. 'A Neglected Late 18th Century Organ Treatise.' *B.I.O.S. Journal*, no. 10 (1986).

Scholes, Percy A. *A New Enquiry into the Life and Work of Dr Burney.* London, Proceedings of the Musical Association, Session LXVII, 1941.

The Great Dr Burney. London, New York, Toronto: Oxford University Press, 1948.

Speller, John L. 'Before the First Lesson: A Study of Some Eighteenth-Century Voluntaries in Relation to the Instruments on Which They Were Played.' *B.I.O.S. Journal*, no. 20 (1996), 64–84.

Sutcliffe, W. Dean. 'The Shapes of Sociability in the Instrumental Music of the Later Eighteenth Century.' *Journal of the Royal Musical Association*, vol. 138, no. 1 (2013), 1–45, DOI: www.tandfonline.com/doi/abs/10.1080/02690403.2013.771941

Instrumental Music in an Age of Sociability: Haydn, Mozart and Friends. Cambridge: Cambridge University Press, 2019.

Temperley, Nicholas. 'Organ Music in Parish Churches, 1660–1730.' *B.I.O.S. Journal*, no. 5. Oxford: Positif Press, 1981.

Thistlethwaite, Nicholas. *The Making of the Victorian Organ.* Cambridge: Cambridge University Press, 1990.

Timbs, John. *Curiosities of London.* London: David Rogue, 1867.

Viala, Alain. *La galanterie: une mythologie française.* Paris: Éditions du Seuil, 2019.

Weber, William. 'Did People Listen in the 18th Century?' *Early Music*, no. 25 (1997), 678–91.

Williams, Peter. *A New History of the Organ, from the Greeks to the Present Day.* London & Boston: Faber and Faber, 1980.

'Preface' to *Twelve Voluntaries for Organ or Harpsichord by William Boyce or Maurice Green.* London: Galliard Limited, 1969.

Acknowledgements

The origin of this study goes back to my doctoral thesis, written in French and submitted at La Sorbonne, Paris, in 1997: *L'orgue dans la société anglaise au XVIIIème siècle: éthique et esthétique de la modération* (Lille: Presses Universitaires du Septentrion, 1997). My interest in the subject has not subsided since I first approached it, and I felt it could make sense to reframe part of my original work and other subsequent papers and make this material available in English in condensed form, while focusing more precisely on the personality and work of Dr Burney. I am grateful to Jacques Carré, Emeritus Professor at Sorbonne University, who supervised my thesis on this slightly unusual topic many years ago. I am also grateful to Dr Christopher Kent, who kindly welcomed me at the beginning of my research, introduced me to the work of the British Institute of Organ Studies (to whom I also owe a debt of gratitude) and was a member of the board of examiners when I submitted my thesis. My thanks extend to Dr David Ponsford, with whom I share so many interests and the same passion for organs (both French and English), and who kindly reread the first draft of this study and helped me to improve it. I claim full responsibility, however, for whatever errors or stylistic clumsiness I may have overlooked. Finally, I want to thank my editor, Professor Simon P. Keefe, for his support, the librarians at the Bodleian Library who kindly helped me over many successive summers, and William Vann, Organist and Director of Music, Royal Hospital Chelsea, who has kindly provided a photograph of the organ at the Royal Hospital.

Cambridge Elements ☰

Elements in Music and Musicians 1750–1850

Simon P. Keefe
University of Sheffield, UK

About the Series

Music and Musicians, 1750-1850 explores musical culture in the late eighteenth and early nineteenth centuries through individual, cutting-edge studies (c. 30,000 words) that imaginatively re-think a period traditionally associated with high classicism and early romanticism. The series interrogates images and reputations, composers, instruments and performers, critical and aesthetic ideas, travel and migration, and music and social upheaval (including wars and conflicts), thereby demonstrating the cultural vibrancy of the period. Through discussion of musicians' interactions with one another and with non-musicians, real-world experiences in and outside music, evolving reputations, and little studied career contexts and environments, Music and Musicians, 1750-1850 works across the conventional 'silos' of composer, genre, style, and place, as well as in many instances across the (notional) 1800 divide. All contributions appeal to a wide readership of scholars, students, practitioners and informed musical public.

Cambridge Elements ☰

Elements in Music and Musicians 1750–1850

Elements in the Series

Dr Charles Burney and the Organ
Pierre Dubois

A full series listing is available at: www.cambridge.org/eimm

Printed in the United States
by Baker & Taylor Publisher Services